Making Sense of Behavior

The Meaning of Control

William T. Powers

D1274977

PUBLISHED BY

Benchmark Publications Inc.
65 Locust Avenue - P.O. Box 1594
New Canaan, Connecticut 06840-1594

Making Sense of Behavior - The Meaning of Control
by William T. Powers

Cover design by John Williams

ISBN 0-09647121-5-6

05 04 03 02 01 00 99 98   5 4 3 2 1

Contents

About the Author

Mr. Powers' interest in control theory began when he was a junior medical physicist at the Argonne Cancer Research Hospital in Chicago during the early 1950s. Since then he has carried on dual careers; an official one as a designer of electronic systems for science, medicine, and commerce, and an unofficial one as an explorer of the organization of living systems. Now retired with his wife Mary in Durango, Colorado, he continues his work on living systems through a busy discussion group on the internet, through designing computer models of living control systems, and through meetings and conferences on his favorite subject. He has published numerous articles in scientific and technical journals as well as several books, of which this is the fourth. He says,

"I have finally figured out what I want to be when I grow up: dead."

Foreword

Humans find humans endlessly fascinating. Alexander Pope was more pontifical about it: "The proper study of mankind is man." Since you have opened this book, no doubt you have a similar sentiment, and no doubt you have already read many books and uncounted magazine articles about the nature of humankind. If you are a scholar of some years, you have read hundreds, even thousands. What can still another book promise?

For almost a century, it has been the custom among American psychologists to seek to understand human nature by watching what people *do*. Most books about human nature focus on human doings; they focus on nameable acts with beginnings and endings. Consider a television set. What does a TV do? It shows us moving pictures on its screen; that is the "behavior" we see. But we could spend an entire lifetime studying the action on the screen and never come to understand a thing about how a TV functions. This book does not focus on visible acts. It focuses on perception. It shows us how action comes about if and only if we find a discrepancy between what we are experiencing and what we want to experience.

In other books, authors who are concerned about morality tell us about good and bad actions, authors who care about influencing others tell us about actions we can take (so they think) to cause others to do what we want them to do, authors who care about the sheer drama of human action tell us tales of derring-do, and so on. Novelists, dramatists, historians, anthropologists, sociologists, psychologists, and others of many stripes describe and catalog for us the multifarious and unending parade of human behavior. It is not surprising that our fascination focuses on action, since visible, tangible action is what we easily perceive. But that focus cannot tell us how any human individual *functions*.

Some books do tell us about perceiving. Artists write about how we see things, musicians about how we hear things, and psychologists and physiologists about how we perceive the energies that impinge upon our sensory organs. A few authors tell us about how we compare things, too. Psychophysicists tell us how sensory illusions affect the comparisons we make—for example, how lines of equal length can look unequal if the eye is misled by other lines angling past them. Many sorts of writers tell us how rich people feel poor in comparison to people still richer.

There is, however, something important missing from all those books, especially those written by psychologists and other social scientists. Very few books tell us how action, perception, and comparison are inescapably intertwined in every action, every thought, every judgment, every yearning. Even fewer tell us how humans *can* function as they do in acting, perceiving, and comparing. Books tell us that humans *do* act, perceive, and compare, but almost no book tells us *how it is possible* for humans and other living creatures to do those things, and how, indeed, all three must always be done simultaneously if they are to be done at all. Do you know of a book, for example, that tells you how a human can stand upright? How is it that we *can* manage, as a wind pushes on us, as we move to wave at someone, as we find ourselves walking along the aisle of a moving bus, as we stand on the deck of a wallowing ship, and as our muscles tire, to remain upright instead of toppling over, as you would naturally expect a mere assembly of loosely joined bones and yielding flesh to do?

I wish psychologists and other social scientists would tell us more about how it is possible for us to maintain what seems to us the "same" perceptions even while the actual energies coming to our sense organs change. How is it, for example, that we can carry a yellow sweater from the bright sunshine into a blue-painted room (where most of the light now falling on the sweater will be far bluer than the sunshine) and still believe the sweater to have the same color it had outside in the sunshine? And how is it, though we can be continually conscious of our own unceasing movements and the unceasing flow of movement in the world around us, that we can nevertheless somehow mark off in our imaginations this moment and that moment and say that an event—that is, some separable thing—has happened between those moments? Such questions could be treated only superficially until William T. Powers showed us the necessary neural hierarchy. I wish, too, that psychologists and other social scientists would tell us more about goals and purposes—about the ways our actions can carry us toward states of affairs we want but do not yet have. When we get distracted from our purposes, as we do repeatedly, every day, how is it that we can repeatedly return to those previous purposes instead of staying with the new direction into which the distraction (so some would think) has sent us? Few research psychologists deal with purposes, though industrial psychologists give lots of advice to managers (but not much to workers) about how to achieve their purposes.

I also wish some books would notice the fact that we use constantly *varying* actions to maintain *unvarying* states—as when we maintain our bodies upright. Very few modern books on psychology notice that fact, though fiction writers seem well aware of it. Finally, I wish the books would not merely speculate on how these marvels can come about, but would tell us how to make a real, tangible, working model that will maintain a desired state despite unpredictable disturbances to it—a model, in other words, that will function in the same way a living creature functions. The only writings I know that tell us how to make such a model, that tell us about actual models that have been built and that do indeed function that way, are the writings of William T. Powers and those of other researchers who have learned from him how to do it—writings, that is, about Perceptual Control Theory.

I have listed some deficiencies of the great bulk of books written without attention to Perceptual Control Theory, and I have mentioned some particular questions with which they cannot cope. But the great contribution to the life sciences brought by Powers and his colleagues is far more than giving appealing explanations of particular phenomena. All the books do that much—or try to do so. The great thing a researcher can do with Perceptual Control Theory (and that we onlookers can do, too) is to return to the fundamental faith of science—to the principle that a function or effect possible or necessary at one place and time must be possible or necessary at all places and all times. If you find that this human sees a rapid series of slightly differing still pictures as a moving picture, then every human who is physically normal must also see this "flicker fusion," or we must not accept the phenomenon as being one of the ways in which the human animal functions. The principle does not allow us to be satisfied if most but not all humans perceive flicker fusion, or if a great many people "tend" to see it, or if everyone in South America sees it. A science of the functioning of living creatures must be willing to test its claims on *every* individual who comes along. The underlying axioms of Perceptual Control Theory and its success in experimentation enable us to return to that strict criterion. The experiments that have been done by Powers, Marken, Bourbon, Robertson, McClelland, Plooij, Herschberger and McPhail demonstrate that psychologists can now cease offering such excuses as "behavior is by nature probabilistic." We can now accept the same standard used in physics and chemistry.

This book is a brief, nonmathematical summary of the lifework of William T. Powers. Here he puts succinctly his current theorizing after several decades of thinking, experimenting, and coping with the challenges of skeptics, both friendly and hostile. *Studies in PCT*, in the Reference section of this book, tells how to find further and more technical information.

In the pursuit of the science of living things, these are great and perilous times. We are at a crisis, a turning point. Long-standing beliefs are showing fatal flaws. Long and honorable careers are threatened. It has become unmistakably clear to everyone who has actually put a hand to a working model that Perceptual Control Theory brings us not merely a few unusual notions, not merely a "viewpoint," but a sea-change, a paradigm shift. It is thrilling to participate in this astonishing and ardently welcome revolution, even in the smallest way.

Philip J. Runkel
Eugene, Oregon
August, 1997

Philip J. Runkel is Professor Emeritus of Education and of Psychology at the University of Oregon. For 35 years, he has taught and written in the fields of social psychology, school organization, research method, statistics, and organizational consulting. His work as an organizational consultant to schools began in 1968. His publications include *Research on Human Behavior: A Systematic Guide to Method* (with Joseph E. McGrath), *Handbook of Organization Development in Schools* (3rd edition, with Richard A. Schmuck), several other books, and several dozen articles and chapters.

Preface

This is a book about human nature, as we try to guess about it by watching human behavior. It's about a particular theory that seems to fit a great deal of what we see people doing and a great deal of our own private experience. A lot of people think that this is a pretty good theory.

But my object in this book is not to persuade you that the theory is right, either by itself or by comparison with other theories. My main objective is to tell you what the theory is and why it has been constructed as it is. I will tell you of the observations that I have thought needed an explanation, and of how this theory appears to explain them. You can decide for yourself whether the theory and the observations go together, and are important.

I'm writing this book as I would write to a friend, not as I would write to impress the editorial board of a scientific publication. Behind the theory you will find here is a considerable technical background and a few dozen papers in the scientific literature, but I assume that most readers won't care about that. My aim is for you to understand the theory, which my colleagues and I call "Perceptual Control Theory" or "PCT" for short. No technical background is needed; the basic facts and relationships you must understand are part of ordinary life, and I suspect that you already understand them. If you remember a little of your high-school algebra, that's wonderful, but you won't need it here.

There are places where you can read more in depth about PCT; a bibliography at the end of the book will give you an entry. While I'll try to avoid saying anything that contradicts a more detailed discussion of PCT, I'm thinking here only of people just getting started, who know little or nothing about it and aren't technically inclined. So I'll keep the discussion as simple and direct as possible, although not any more simple and direct than that. I am assuming that I'm talking to an intelligent layperson willing to put out a little effort to understand something new. If that sounds like a good contract, we can proceed.

A lot of people have helped me toward writing this book, not the least of whom are Perry and Fred Good, who nagged me into doing it, and Dag Forssell, whose efforts in supporting PCT have been expressed in many practical and time-consuming ways, the final form of this book being just one example of many. In addition, many people in the Control Systems Group, which is devoted to PCT, and on an Internet discussion group called CSGnet, have forced me to learn how to say what I mean more clearly, and some of them have offered detailed critiques of this book as it was in progress. Any list would be incomplete, but I am immediately (and randomly) mindful of Dick Robertson, Tom Bourbon, Phil Runkel, Rick Marken, Greg Williams, the Bruces Abbott and Gregory, Kent McClelland, Martin Taylor, Bill Leach… and I will stop the list there because the longer it gets, the more embarrassing it will be when I realize which respected colleagues I have left out.

But I will not leave out my wife Mary, who against all reason has loved me, trusted me, and helped me through all the 40 years of development behind PCT, and who now grows old with me, a respected teacher of PCT in her own right.

And with that, let us dive right into our subject with Chapter One.

Bill Powers
Durango, Colorado
May, 1997

Chapter 1

Controlling

*In which we explore a
closed circle of causation
that is involved in all
control processes*

Controlling

Perceptual Control Theory is about controlling. It's not about responding to stimuli, or planning actions and then carrying them out; it's not about effects of traumatic incidents on later behavior; it's not about particular things people do under particular circumstances. It's not about attitudes or habits or beliefs or tendencies. It's not about predicting. It's just about one kind of behavior that we can see people carrying out, called controlling.

Controlling is important because in the natural world only living organisms can do it. Many things in the nonliving world respond when things happen to them—a baseball hit by a bat flies enthusiastically through the air; a mousetrap responds to a touch by snapping shut. Many things in the nonliving world show complex patterns of behavior—iron filings on a card leap into arcs and loops when a magnet is brought underneath the card; stars form from dust and gas in a galaxy and go through complex life cycles ending in gigantic bangs or dark and silent whimpers. Nonliving things even reproduce themselves, as when a seed crystal in a solution creates an ever-growing tree of crystals of the same kind.

But none of these nonliving things can control anything. None of them can change their actions on something else to make the outcome repeat or remain the same in a changing environment. None of them can have or carry out intentions concerning what is to happen to them. Controlling is a unique process, unique to life (except, of course, for artificial control systems, built by living ones to imitate their behavior).

It's therefore important to understand this process called controlling, and that is what we will spend the first part of this book doing.

There are three basic functions that controlling requires: action, perception, and comparison. Let's take them up one at a time (although it's impossible to speak about *only* one at a time).

Action

If a person is to control something, the person has to be able to affect whatever it is that is to be controlled. Affecting it requires some sort of action that involves the use of muscles or glands. Much of controlling requires producing an action that has an effect on the physical environment. Much action requires producing internal effects that nobody else can see, as in swallowing. Among all the effects that a given action might have, the only immediately pertinent one is an effect that changes the thing being controlled.

There's a difference between merely affecting something and controlling it. You can affect the path of a car going down the road by turning the steering wheel, but to control the path of the car you have to have a particular effect, not just any effect. Turning the wheel has to keep the car on the road rather than running it into a wall or an oncoming truck. Of course the car could be steered into the wall or the truck; it's all a matter of which possible effect is to be controlled.

The interesting thing about controlling something is that *you can't plan the actions needed for control beforehand.* When you take a bath, you can't just plan out how much to turn the hot and cold faucet handles and then execute the plan. If you do that, the bath is going to end up too hot or too cold. You have to be willing to turn the faucet handles whichever way is needed: If the water is getting too hot, you turn on more cold water or less hot water. It's the same for steering a car; you can't plan the steering wheel movements in advance. If a little wind blows the car too far to the left, you have to turn the wheel right; there's no choice if you want the car to stay on the road. But unless you have some stupendous secret way of predicting the weather all the way down to the local wind velocity and direction at 10:07 A.M. tomorrow, you are simply going to have to wait for 10:07 A.M. tomorrow to see which way and by how much you end up turning the steering wheel, if at all. So controlling can't be about planning actions.

The reason it can't is that the world is not really as consistent and predictable as it seems to be. Winds blow, bumps in the road pass under your wheels, objects move around, your own body doesn't go exactly where you expect, and each little error adds to previous errors cumulatively. The temperature of water in the pipes is always changing, just with time or because other people are using the same water supply. One door sticks when another swings free; one door is heavy and another is light. When you pick up a glass to take a sip of beer, the glass is lighter the next time you pick it up. When you reach for your socks in the morning, they're never in exactly the same place or oriented with the heels on the same side.

We think that our lives are full of repetitive and familiar actions, but to say that we do "the same thing" every day is only a way of speaking. When we brush our teeth, get dressed, eat breakfast, drive or take a bus to work, deal with customers or bosses, return home, eat dinner, watch TV, and go to bed, we probably never produce the same actions two days in a row. What we're doing is causing certain *controlled consequences of action* to repeat, but the only way we can manage to do that is to *change* our actions exactly as required in the brand-new world that we encounter every minute of the day.

Human actions that we can see from outside a person are tremendously variable; it is *only their consequences* that repeat, more or less. But if actions were not variable, if they did not vary exactly as they do vary, in detail, the same consequences couldn't possibly repeat. The reason is that the world itself shows a lot of variation, and for every variation, our actions have to vary in the opposite way if any particular consequence of acting is to occur again and again. *Controlling means producing repeatable consequences by variable actions.*

Perception

A funny scene that moviemakers often use shows us a driver and a passenger in a car, driving down a crowded street. The driver is chatting away to the passenger at a great rate, eyes fixed firmly on the passenger, while the passenger looks in horror at the double-parked buses and oncoming trucks into which the car is doomed to plow in the next second. Both the passenger and the audience are thinking, *"For God's sake, look at the road!"*

In studies of driving behavior, it's been observed that men will look away from the road (in light traffic or none) for perhaps one and a half seconds before looking back; women a little longer. Apparently, being able to perceive where the car is relative to its environment is considered fairly important in driving. All the moviemaker has to do is stretch out the time the driver isn't looking at the road to four or five seconds, and every driver in the audience will start tensing up.

Obviously, perception is important for control. But what is perception? It's only what our senses tell us about the world. It's some sort of representation in our brains of what is going on outside us and inside us, a report on the status of things that exist or are happening. Most of what we perceive isn't involved in control—watching the moon rise, observing the leaves of trees blowing in the wind, seeing a football player score a goal, contemplating the same old mess in the garage. Perception is a passive taking-in, an input. What does it have to do with acting on the world?

To repeat, why should perception be so important for control? It's not needed for turning the steering wheel as the car careens around the hairpin turns on a mountain road—you could do that blindfolded, couldn't you? Your muscles are still working. Sometimes you do things without using perception, like tossing your coat toward a chair without looking, but those are cases where the outcome isn't very important. When you're planning to step into a bathtub, you don't just turn the faucet handles by a particular amount, wait for the tub to fill, and step in. You *feel* the water temperature, and keep feeling it and adjusting the faucet handles so the temperature will be just right when you commit your defenseless skin to full immersion. When you drive a car, particularly in traffic or on a mountain road, you look where you're going almost continuously. On that twisty mountain road with cars coming around every blind corner you don't look away for even *one second*.

The general rule is that if you want to control something, you have to perceive it. This doesn't mean just perceiving that something exists, as in looking out the windshield and noticing that there's a road out there. It means perceiving exactly the aspect of the world that is supposed to be under control. You don't care what color the road is or whether it's four lanes wide or six; when you're trying to stay in your lane, you're looking at the relationship of the front of the car to the lane, and trying to keep that visual picture in a certain configuration that you know means you're in your lane. You can't do that blindfolded; you can't do it without watching what's going on nearly all the time. When you're filling your bath, you don't just perceive that the water looks wet and sloshy; you specifically use your temperature sensors to report on the current temperature of the water because that's what you're controlling, temperature.

Perception tells us the current status of whatever it is we're trying to control. Without that information, received continuously or at frequent intervals, we can't control anything. Perception is just as important as action, for controlling.

Comparison and Error

Suppose a driver is whizzing along the highway and notices that the front of the car is about six inches from the ditch and getting closer. The driver's action of turning the steering wheel has put the car in that position, and the driver perceives it in that position. The question that naturally comes to mind is, "So what?"

If everything continues as it is going, the driver's perceptions will faithfully report the overlap of the edge of the ditch by the car's fender, then a tilt of the world as the car slides into the ditch, then the world upside down, then rightside up, accompanied by various sharp blows reported by other senses, until whatever the result is has finished happening. What is missing from this picture?

What is missing is the difference between what the driver *is* perceiving and what the driver would far prefer to be perceiving. When you learn to drive, the first thing you learn after getting the car into motion is how the road should look relative to the front of the car as you see it from the driver's seat. Somehow this image remains in your head and as you drive along you are continually comparing how the scene *does* look with how it *should* look. If the way it does look is shifted to the right of how it should look, you turn the wheel leftward until there is a match again. A left shift leads to a rightward turn of the wheel. Once you learn this relationship it becomes automatic; you don't have to think it out any more. You have constructed an automatic control system that will, as long as you're looking, keep the actual perception matching the appearance you know it should have. When you do that, the car settles down into its lane and stays there. The "appearance you know it should have" is called a reference perception, or reference condition, or reference state because it is with reference to this internal information that you judge the perception as too little, too much, or just right; too far left, too far right, or dead on; too hot, too cold, or perfect. If differences exist, we call them "errors" in PCT. Error doesn't mean "blunder" or "mistake"; it just means a *difference between what is being perceived and what is intended to be perceived.*

You get something else free: If a crosswind springs up, or the road tilts, or you hit a bump, or a front tire goes soft, the car will tend to veer to one side. But that will cause a difference, an error, between the position of the road that you perceive and the reference picture you carry in your head for how the road *should* look. The same little automatic control system, comparing the real perception with the reference perception, will turn the wheel the opposite way, resisting and in fact correcting the effect of the disturbance, any disturbance, without any instruction to do so. You may be listening to the radio or talking to your passenger, and not even notice what this simple control system is so kindly doing for you—as long as you keep one eye on the road.

Two pieces of information are needed for the comparison process: the actual state (as perceived) of whatever is being controlled, and the target or goal state for that perception that is intended or desired, the reference perception. This reference perception or target is also called an *intention*. The picture of the car in its lane that you carry in your head is the picture you *intend* to perceive (If you've been reading philosophy, you may know some other meanings for the word *intention*. While you're reading this book, please forget them. We're talking about the first meaning that my dictionary gives: the act of determining that some event or result will occur).

So intentions come into control. Intentions define what *is to be brought into experience or is to continue to be experienced.* This is not quite the same as predicting what is going to happen. When you make a prediction, you assume that the events that follow the prediction are caused by natural laws or the behavior of other things and people over which you have no control, including what you have already done yourself. A gambler predicts that the dice will show a six on the next throw. But if the gambler has control of the dice, the other players will not treat the bet as a prediction; they will treat it as cheating. They will find the electromagnet under the table and throw it and the gambler out into the street, if he is lucky.

When you control something like the path of a car, you have continuously in mind some particular conception of the right position in the lane. This picture of the right path isn't like a prediction; it's like a target or a blueprint. The way the car is traveling can be compared continuously with the way it is supposed to be traveling, and the steering wheel can be moved all during the trip to keep the car where it is supposed to be in its lane. Even if you aren't conscious of the reference image at all, you still know when the actual image is wrong and when it's right. *Something* knows about the reference image.

There is no prediction involved in the destination of the trip; that is normally known all during the trip. If a road is closed, the car is not deflected to some other destination; the steering wheel is turned to steer the car by whatever routes are open until it reaches the intended destination. Even though many unpredictable problems can arise as a driver goes to work, one would be well advised to bet that the car will get there by *some* means.

When you fill the bath, you have in mind a particular temperature that you want to feel. If the temperature you feel is higher than that, you add cold water or reduce the hot water input; if lower, you do the opposite. While the bath fills you are continuously or repeatedly doing this comparison, and continuously or repeatedly acting to maintain a match between the actual perception and the reference perception. You aren't *predicting* that the temperature will be right; you're *making* it be right, by controlling it.

Obviously, the result of comparison is information about a difference or error between actual and reference perceptions, and this information is the basis for the action that corrects the difference.

Circular Causation

One reason that control was not recognized as a special phenomenon long ago is that it seems to do violence to cause and effect. Psychology and biology, when trying to be sciences, have always tried to follow the lead of physics, and in physics no object behaves unless something else makes it behave by pushing on it or otherwise having some effect on it. Engineering also suggested the same thing; classical machines moved only as they were made to move by flowing or falling water, expanding steam, blowing wind, or unwinding springs. Any object, Isaac Newton said, continues in a state of rest or uniform motion unless acted upon by some external force. For most behavioral sciences that was a good enough concept on which to found a science of animal and human behavior.

As a result, when psychologists and biologists looked for explanations of behavior, they looked at the environment surrounding an organism. Blow a puff of air onto a person's bare eyeball, and the person will blink almost every time. Stick a pin into someone and the person will often yell "OUCH!" and will most likely jerk away from the pin. Show a person a picture of a tasty dessert, and the person (according to people who sell advertising) will probably salivate and rush to the store to buy some. Treat a child badly, and the child will (if you believe everything you read) quite often grow up to rob convenience stores. So the problem of explaining behavior, as well as predicting and controlling it, became simply a problem of finding out how people typically react to the forces, literal or figurative, applied to them by their environments. If you want to control behavior, all you have to do is find out which parts of the environment are causing the behavior, and manipulate the environment.

This is how the sciences of behavior started out thinking about behavior, but while these ideas were forming there were dissenters who saw something else going on.

The chief problem with explaining behavior in terms of environmental causes has always been that we can see more behavior than causes. It's all very well to call every behavior a "response," but unless you can pair up some specific stimulus with each response, that is more an assertion of faith than an observation. The opponents of the environmental-causation principle could show innumerable examples of actions for which no stimulus, no external cause, can be found—apparently spontaneous behavior, such as Beethoven's composing his 5th Symphony. More specifically, many examples could be found in which a person acted as if toward some predetermined end, as in the way one drives a car to Philadelphia. It is very difficult to point to the environmental causes that explain why each car converging on Philadelphia on any given day is being driven in that direction instead of some other. The best you can do is guess there's something about Philadelphia that stimulates drivers to go in that direction. And you would make that guess only if you already believed that all behavior had to be explained by something in the environment.

The idea of spontaneous behavior was criticized, ridiculed, and opposed with violently emotional arguments by those who called themselves scientists. Even St. Thomas Aquinas had insisted that nothing moves of itself in the natural world. The only Prime Mover Unmoved was God, and everything else in the universe moved because something else made it move. On this principle, if on few others, science and religion agreed.

The arguments for spontaneous behavior were as primitive as the arguments against it, and what's more, they didn't capture more than half of the real difficulty that the then-scientific pundits had to face. The problem is not simply that we can find examples of behavior that seem spontaneous, but that we can find kinds of behavior that literally *cause themselves*.

Consider your bath again. When you feel the incoming water temperature, the heat you feel could be interpreted as a stimulus causing you to turn the cold water faucet handle in the direction that lets more cold water in. But as you turn the faucet handle, the temperature you are feeling is caused to fall, so the new temperature that you feel is caused by turning the cold-water handle. After this goes on a while, the water entering the tub has come to a new temperature and the faucet handle-turning has stopped.

So we can trace cause and effect all the way around a closed circle. The temperature of the water causes you to change the handle angle, and changing the handle angle causes the temperature of the water to change. There is no outside agency making you turn the handle; the water temperature would not change unless you did turn the handle. This little closed loop of causality seems to have an existence of its own; it operates independently of anything going on outside it, and it results in the water temperature changing from a starting value to a final value, for no apparent reason.

Whenever this kind of situation came up, in which tracing cause and effect bent the chain of reasoning into a circle, arguments started and confusion spread among psychologists and philosophers. Ordinary logic simply couldn't handle it because ordinary logic demanded that causes come before effects and that they be independent of effects. The final temperature of the bathwater didn't exist before the handle-turning occurred, and being part of the future, couldn't affect the present handle-turning. If the temperature of the water caused handle-turning, it couldn't at the same time be an effect of handle-turning: When it comes to cause and effect, you have to choose sides and stick with your choice.

It took behavioral scientists a very long time to get this traumatic problem sorted out; in most quarters they are still having problems with it. Echoes of all the old arguments can still be heard in the halls of ivy. We needn't go through all those old arguments, and indeed will be better off ignoring them because they have confused better minds than mine or yours. If we concentrate on understanding how this closed circle of causation works, we can develop a basis from which anyone can look back on the old arguments and see what they missed, if anyone wants to take the time to rehash history.

The closed circle of causation is the heart of the kind of behavior we call controlling. In the first parts of this chapter, we went through the basic processes of action, perception, and comparison that give us a rough idea of how systems like this work. We saw that the final effect produced by one of these causal loops was determined not by the environment, but by something we are calling a reference condition, something inside the person that defines a particular state of a perception and sets it up as a target or an intention against which actual perceptions are to be matched. We saw how a comparison of actual and reference perceptions leads to information about the difference, and how the difference leads to actions that affect the world in the way needed to eliminate the difference, to correct the error. So even without putting up a red flag, we were talking about a closed causal loop.

It should be apparent by now that if we just accept what we observe and experience and try to understand it, ignoring all the other theories and guesses and principles that people have used to explain how these kinds of behavior work, we can begin to comprehend controlling as a real and basically simple process. If, as your understanding grows, you start to wonder how such a simple explanation could possibly have been overlooked during the whole history of the behavioral sciences, I can only say that once you get a wrong concept in your head, it is very hard to see through it.

Anyway, this idea really hasn't been overlooked; many scientists and philosophers have in one way or another seen circular causality and intentional behavior as having basic importance. They just weren't considered to be in the mainstream of science.

Chapter 2

Perceptual Control

In which we see that behavior is the process by which we act on the world to control perceptions that matter to us

Perceptual Control

Perception plays a central role in controlling. This is why the theory behind this book is called Perceptual Control Theory, or PCT. The emphasis in PCT is not only to understand control from an outside observer's point of view, as in engineering control theory, but to grasp how control appears to the controller—that is, to you and me, who occupy our own copies of this marvelous mechanism and participate in running it. Taking this point of view gives us a new slant on perception. But first, let's look at the most usual concept of perception, one that has caused many difficulties.

The External View of Perception

When we look at another person, we can see that person's body movements and the effects of those movements on the person and the environment. But we can't see the other person's perceptions. From neurology we know that there are sensory receptors in the person's eyes, skin, ears, joints, muscles, viscera, and mucous membranes, and that each tiny sensory ending generates nerve signals when the environment stimulates it. These nerve signals converge into the lower parts of the brain, where they give rise to more neural signals in a series of steps going upward through the brain to the highest levels. Logically, we know that all of human experience must be carried by these signals, these perceptual signals, including the experiences that are occurring right now as we read these words. So from this external point of view, it seems there is a physical body and a physical environment, with the other person's perceptions of those things existing invisibly inside the other person's brain.

This point of view is useful for constructing models of behavior and of the brain's functions. We use such models, as far as we can construct them with today's knowledge, in PCT, as many others use them in constructing and testing other theories about the brain and behavior. When using these models we treat the nerve-signals in the brain as representing things outside the brain; intensities, shapes, movements, events, relationships, and much more. Psychology itself began with "psychophysics," an attempt to find relationships between physical measures of the outside world and the subjective experiences we have of that world (which we would now identify with the neural processes in the brain that represent the outside world).

When we try to transfer this picture of perception to ourselves, however, we are led straight into an intellectual error. Since you probably have at least one of your hands readily available, we can use it to illustrate the problem.

Look at your hand. There it is, with fingers and skin and wrinkles. You can wiggle the fingers, turn the hand palm up and palm down, make a fist. As you do these things, you are, of course perceiving that they are happening. So you can see your hand and what it is doing—but where is the *perception* of your hand? If you take the externalized neurological point of view, you will say that the perception of the hand must be somewhere inside you, behind your eyes and nose, under your hair, and above your neck: in your head.

Unfortunately, it's hard to see those perceptions because you can't see inside your head any more than you can see inside someone else's head. You know, intellectually, that those nerve-signals must be there because you can't be the only person in the world who has no brain. Seeing how perception works in other people—and there is lots of neurological evidence to show that perception does depend on nerve signals in all human beings—you have to admit that it probably works the same way in you. But for you, or me, or anyone else, that knowledge is strictly theoretical. We have no direct way to check it out.

I hope I have succeeded in diverting your attention away from your hand for a moment, and that you've been enticed into trying to imagine those ghostly perceptions inside your own head. If you've been doing that, your hand, the real hand you were looking at before, may have receded into the background. You're not trying to understand the hand, but your own inner perception of it, in that place inside your head where you have to feel your way as through a darkened room. A lot of people have felt their way through that darkened room in search of perception.

The Internal View of Perception

If you will attend once again to that hand, you may notice that we have been ignoring a problem. If you can't see your perceptions, but you *can* see your hand, how do you know there is a hand there? I mean literally *how*? When you looked into your own head, where all those neural signals are supposed to be, you didn't see any signals *or* any hand. But when you look at the hand, there it is. You must have some way of knowing about the hand directly, that doesn't depend on neural signals! If you agree that this is true, you will be in good company; even some scientists believe that we can have knowledge of things outside us without having to rely on neural signals. This, of course, is a great mystery because when we study other people, they seem to depend entirely on the presence of neural signals to perceive things outside them. If a person's optic nerve ceases to function for any reason, that person becomes blind. That person can't hold up a hand and see its skin, fingernails, and wrinkles without using neural signals. But apparently, we can. That is extremely odd.

It is so odd, in fact, that we have to conclude that it's wrong. *What's* wrong? The idea that we can know about anything outside us without the aid of neural signals. Therefore, let's just accept that even our own perception works the way it seems to work when neurologists poke around inside people's brains: no neural signals, no perceptions. That leaves us only one explanation of how you know that hand is out there.

The hand you're looking at has to be made of neural signals. There's no other explanation that works. What you're experiencing is not the object outside of you, but a set of neural signals representing something outside of you. You don't need to look inside your head to find perceptions: *When you look at your hand, you're already looking at them.* You're directly experiencing the signals in your brain that represent the world outside you. There is no second way to know about the skin, the wrinkles, the fingernails, the palm, and so on. There is only one way, through neural signals, and you're looking right at them.

From inside yourself, the only place you can be, you have a unique view of your own perceptions that *nobody else in the world can have*. The way these signals appear to human awareness is not as a set of neural signals, blips travelling around in the brain. They appear simply as the way the world looks to you. When a neurosurgeon sticks a probe into your informed-consented brain, he sees only a voltage or a series of blips on an oscilloscope or strip chart; that is how perceptual signals look to an electronic device. But to you, the aware entity in your brain, the very same brain activities look like a hand, an arm supporting the hand, a glass being held by the hand, a room, a world, a universe.

Vision provides a great many perceptions, but let's not forget all the others: touch, smell, hearing, and many more. When that image of your hand moves close enough to an image of another object, you suddenly feel a touch: that's a neural signal, too. When you make the hand squeeze into a fist, you experience the pressure on the skin, the efforts in the muscles of the forearm, the coolness or warmth of your fingertips against your palm. More neural signals. When the hand grasps a glass of water, you feel the contact, the shape, the temperature of the glass. When you lift the glass, you can see the motion, and also feel the changing angles of your joints at shoulder, elbow, and wrist. When you drink the water, you can feel the rim of the glass against your lips, the flow of water over your tongue, the efforts of swallowing and the sensations of water exiting from the world of neural sensations into (you presume) your stomach. You can hear the clink as you set the glass back onto the table. All these experiences are your awareness of neural signals.

When others watch you take a drink of water, they think they're seeing what you're doing. But they see the backs of your fingers curled around the glass, which you don't see; they see the glass tilt away from them toward your mouth, but you see only its rim tilting toward you. They experience nothing of the smoothness, hardness, weight, or temperature of the glass, or how the rim tastes. They see your throat working, but experience nothing of the water in your mouth or the swallowing efforts or the sensations of liquid going down the tube. Most of the experiences you are having are invisible to them; most of what they see happening is invisible to you.

Whenever anyone watches another person behaving, most of what that other person is experiencing goes unobserved. *What little is observed is observed from the wrong point of view.* We come closest to understanding what another person is doing when we try to imagine doing the same things ourselves; when we try to put ourselves inside the other's skin, seeing through the other's eyes, feeling and hearing and tasting with the other's senses. Then we can bring our own experiences to the understanding, and realize that more is going on than the outside observer can possibly see.

Perception, for any one person, is simply the world of experience. This world appears to be partly in a place we call "outside," and partly in a place we call "inside"—that is, inside our own bodies, although still outside the place from which we observe. And, to get to the point, when we *control* something, what we control, necessarily, is one or more of the perceptions that make up this world of experience. Our only view of the real world is our view of the neural signals that represent it, inside our own brains. When we act to make a perception change toward a more desirable state—when we make the perception of the glass change from "on the table" to "near the mouth"—we have no direct knowledge of what we are doing to the reality that is the origin of our neural signals; we know only the final result, how the result looks, feels, smells, sounds, tastes, and so forth.

This is why we say in PCT that behavior is the process by which we control our own perceptions. This doesn't mean that we change a perception of an orange into a perception of a bird; it means only that we act on the world to change where the orange is, whether it is in one piece or in slices, whether it is round or squashed, and so on. It means that we produce actions that alter the world of perception, and that we do so specifically to make the state of that world conform to the reference conditions we ourselves have chosen (to the extent we can change the perceptions by our actions).

Since the world we experience is the world of perception, it usually makes little difference whether we say we're controlling perceptions or controlling the state of the real world. It does, however, make a difference when we try to explain behavior in terms of some physical model of a behaving system. When we do that, we have to stand with one foot in each viewpoint; we construct an objective model as if our own perceptions were exactly the world as it exists, including physics, chemistry, physiology, and neurology. In doing so we explain how it is that another person can be controlling as we observe controlling to occur, using a brain organized as we think it's organized. At the same time, knowing that all experience is experience of neural signals, we are explaining how *we* can control things, and why controlling seems to us the way it seems, and how we can be making up models and theories about controlling.

Half of the jokes in the world are about one person assuming that everyone else sees the world the same way. The husband hangs his new moosehead over the fireplace in the living room and says to his aghast wife, "There, doesn't that look *great?*" The other half of the jokes are about people who are unable to see what everyone else (supposedly) can see—that the wife looking at the moosehead is trying to remember the phone number of her lawyer.

The two problems go together: the problem of reaching agreement with each other about reality, and the problem that all perception is fundamentally private. If our perceptions were not private, we would never disagree with each other about the world and its meanings. If they were not, somehow, similar, we wouldn't be able to tell jokes or communicate about anything. It is, of course, possible that our perceptions are both private and similar. We are all constructed more or less alike, so even if each of us independently develops a system of perceptions of our own, the chances are that what we end up with will not be too radically different from other systems of perception at least in terms of simple matters like light and dark, sweet and salty. But even if we can count on some similarities between perceiving people, we will always remain uncertain about the relationship between human perception in general and the real nature of the world outside us.

I won't pretend that these puzzles about perception and point of view are completely solved by the propositions put forth here. All of this is just my best try at bringing consistency into the study of both publicly observable behavior and private experience. Using the external point of view, we can make objective models that, on a computer, will reproduce some simple forms of human behavior with great precision. Using the internal point of view, we can understand many aspects of behavior by seeing control as control of perception rather than of an objective world. We can make sense not only of other people's behavior, but of our own, using the same concept of perceptual control.

Chapter 3

Levels

*In which we find that control involves
different levels of organization, with
higher control systems inside
a person using lower ones
as the means of control*

Levels

The idea of control of perception sinks in only slowly. At first, it gets in the way of everything. When you reach for a drawer to get a fork, what you've been reading here pops into your head, and you think "That's a perception of a drawer and a perception of a hand reaching toward it; the feeling of pulling the drawer open is a perception; I'm sorting through perceptions of utensils to find a perception of a fork, and now I'm trying to make a perception of my hand with a fork in it...." All this creates a condition of extreme self-consciousness and artificiality. But if you go around hanging the label "perception" on everything you experience, eventually everything will have the same label, and the label will become unimportant. You'll understand that it's all perception the way you understand that your hand has fingers, but most of the time that bit of knowledge will cease to be obtrusive and you can go back, almost, to normal life. Even a baby eventually gets over its fascination with the fact that hands have fingers, although it never forgets this fact.

Our current project, however, requires that we go on paying attention to perception and the way we control it, so we're still on duty and can't relax yet.

Once the basic idea of controlling perceptions starts to feel comfortable, most people come up with the same question. When you start to close your hand to form a fist, you have in mind a state of the hand different from the one you see and feel. You then do whatever it is you do to make the muscles work, and the perceived state of the hand changes until it matches the reference state. The question is about these reference states, conditions, perceptions, signals, whatever you want to call them. Where do they come from?

We can begin to see a general answer by looking at a simple special case. Suppose you want a drink of water. At some point in getting it, you find your hand next to a glass with water in it. The big problem (not now, but certainly at one point in your infant life) is how to use the hand to get the glass where you want it to be (where you want to perceive it to be, of course, but we don't have to keep saying that to the point of being tiresome—let's just agree that it's all perception).

The solution that eventually becomes obvious and then automatic is to place the open hand next to the glass with the palm facing the glass, and then set reference conditions for the curl of the fingers and the sense of pressure against the palm and fingers that clamp the hand firmly enough around the glass to pick it up.

So one answer to the question of what creates reference conditions is "Some other control process being used to control something else." You already have a control system that will curl the fingers together when something specifies a particular configuration of perceptions as a reference condition. So just by specifying the reference conditions that are needed for all the sensations that are involved in controlling hand configuration, you can make this control system create a state of the hand that would be useful for controlling the position of the glass of water. A *hierarchy of control* is suggested, in which one level of control acts by using control systems of a lower level.

In this example of clamping the hand on the glass, where we can stand back coolly and analyze how one control task demands the use of other, subordinate, tasks, it's relatively easy to catch on to the idea of a control hierarchy. That's why I use such an innocuous example. But the real importance of this idea to the human condition is seen only when we consider control of much more important things, like the way you earn money, the principles you think are right, the conceptions you have of society, self, religion, science, and government. At these higher levels we have control systems too, and they are hierarchically related.

When you act to maintain a perception of yourself as an honest person, you do so by choosing principles that you intend to live by, and to live by those principles you act to control procedures, reasoning, and logic that all add up to using the particular principles you have in mind. In trying to discuss a control hierarchy at these lofty levels of perception, there is great danger (I speak from experience) of getting embroiled in arguments about which concepts are the best, which principles are right, which ends justify the methods. All such arguments, while guaranteeing a lively evening, are irrelevant to getting across the *idea* of a control hierarchy, which is the same at any level. So even though it would be more interesting to conduct this discussion at a higher level, the point of the discussion is more likely to get across if we stick to neutral subjects like picking up a glass of water.

We have to take a short break to deal with this word "you" in a sentence like "you set a reference condition." If you, the You to whom I'm talking, knew how to set a reference condition, I wouldn't need to be telling you about any of this. Obviously, *something* is setting the reference condition, and this something is clearly part of you and nobody else, but just as obviously the details are not all available to your consciousness. One reason we make theories is to fill in the blanks where we can't see everything that goes on.

The easiest way around this problem of "you" is to use terms like "the control system" and "it." None of us can see our own nervous systems; we experience only activities in those systems. As far as we are concerned, the nervous system in which we live is an "it", not an "I". What we're trying to do here is to build up a conception, a model, a theory about how this nervous system thing can add up to be ourselves; how it can do what we see it doing in others and in us. When we talk about one little part of this nervous system, we are talking about only one little part of a whole person. The little part is not aware and conscious as the whole is; it does not think as the whole does; it does not have an identity that we could call "you." Each little part performs just one simple function.

So with (or without) your permission, I am going to start talking about control systems inside of you, referring to them as "it" and in general acting as if we're talking about a piece of machinery. The subject of your conscious participation in the operations of these control systems can be put off, although you can form your own judgments about how much of the processes you can actually sense consciously. Not everything to be proposed here is outside awareness, but some parts of it are. I'm sure you will be able to tell the difference. We can put that problem aside for now.

While we're standing around in this coffee break, I should also mention a few things about the problems of a theoretician trying to build a plausible picture of how behavior works—a model that conceivably could be taken as a picture of the real nervous system and its functions. What the theoretician does *not* want is a different theory for every different situation. There are millions of different situations; if we had to have a brand-new explanation for each one, we would never get very far. If we think of a person as just one uniform chunk, then every time we see a new behavior we would have to build a new model to take care of just that one situation.

This is the main reason we try to see *functional units* inside a person, units that always do the same thing in the same way. There are some pretty compelling reasons for thinking that this is the right approach; that the real system, too, is made of functional units that always do the same thing the same way. If that were not true, the entire nervous system would have to be rewired or drastically altered in some way each time the same limbs had to be used for a new purpose, each time the same perception showed up in a new context, each time the world outside changed in any way. This just doesn't seem possible, given what we know about how long it takes for the nervous system to get organized initially, and how long it takes to learn new skills. When you're typing away and pause for a second to push your glasses back up, you can't have reorganized all the connections from your brain to your muscles just for that one act—and then have reorganized back again to type the next word.

In the background of this discussion is the idea that we are looking for small general-purpose units of organization which can become parts of larger units, which in turn can become parts of still larger units. The discussion is not going to stay for very long on the simple units; there are other sources you can look up (bibliography at the end of the book) if you really want to get into more detail. The point here is only to establish a certain concept of *hierarchical* control, and to present a general notion of the whole brain as being composed of a large number of functional units, each carrying out one specialized control process and all together adding up to a whole real human being. This is not necessarily the picture that science will eventually agree upon, but it is a very fruitful starting point.

OK, coffee break's over.

What sets the reference condition for the control system that configures the hand that is next to the glass of water? Another control system at a higher level of organization. The reference condition for the second control system specifies a particular relationship between the hand and the glass: hand grasping glass. This second control system, however, cannot bypass the control systems that are already using the muscles to curl the fingers, rotate the hand, and regulate sensed pressure on the skin. Those control systems are always connected and always working. If the second or higher-level control system tried to send commands directly to the muscles, the lower-level control systems would sense changes in the hand configuration and apply corrective commands to the same muscles, canceling the command from the higher system.

The only way the second-level control system can operate on its world is by adjusting the reference conditions for the first set of control systems. The relationship is much like that between a platoon of soldiers and a drill sergeant. The drill sergeant can't directly operate the soldiers' legs; to get the marchers to turn a corner, the sergeant tells the marchers the direction they are to want to go all by themselves. He tells them politely, "COL'M RAAAAT—HAR!" On hearing this command, the line of soldiers is to turn right one soldier at a time, starting with the lead soldier, as if the column is turning at a street corner. Each soldier, on reaching the corner where the turn is to happen, plants his left foot where the left foot of the soldier ahead was planted two steps ago, and pivots on it to the right (during the same step) while his right leg swings forward ready for the next step in the new direction, exactly as the previous soldier did. It's easy once you learn it. This "column right" command, however, has *no effect* on the muscles of the soldiers or the direction in which they are marching. It is taken in as audible information by the solders' ears and brains and converted to meanings; the meanings are converted into a logical reference condition involving a program that all the soldiers, one hopes, have learned: (1) Continue marching in a straight line. (2) If I am at the corner where the column is turning right, (3a) wait until the left foot contacts the ground, then (3b) pivot right, otherwise (4), go back to (1).

This is just like a computer program. From the moment the sergeant says "march!"—pronounced "HAR!"—each soldier selects a reference program stored in memory and activates it. This program is immediately recognized, and continues to be recognized no matter what part of it is in operation. Even though each soldier was marching—perceived himself or herself to be marching—in a straight line prior to the command, now the same perception has become an element of a program that the soldier recognizes and controls. Since there is an "if" in the program, it's not just a sequence; the straight-line marching will continue until the answer to the "if" question changes. Am I at the corner yet? If no, continue marching. If yes, wait for the left foot to hit the ground and pivot right. This little unit of behavior was first proposed by Miller, Galanter, and Pribram in 1960. They called it the TOTE unit, for "test-operate-test-exit," in their book *Plans and the Structure of Behavior*. The authors tried to make this unit work for all levels of behavior, a proposition with which I take strong issue, but it's still a good book and worth reading three or four decades later.

Since the "HAR" following a command to turn right is always given as the right foot contacts the ground, the lead soldier has about half a second to understand the command, set the reference condition to the right program, perceive that his left foot has hit the ground, and pivot right. The next soldier has about one second and goes several times around the program loop, and so on to the last soldier who may not turn for 10 seconds or more and goes around the program loop many times.

This program does not operate the muscles directly. Instead, the unit of organization that carries out the program sets reference conditions for *sequences of perceptions*. The initial sequence is "left, right, left, right...." Then, at the critical moment, the reference sequence is set to "right, PIVOT RIGHT 90 DEGREES ON LEFT FOOT, right, left" immediately followed by a return to the initial sequence of "right, left, right, left, right...." So the program says "Select sequence A; if condition B is met, select sequence C, otherwise select sequence A."

A *constant* setting of the reference condition for a sequence implies a *continuing pattern of change*. Control of the sequence is accomplished by issuing a series of reference-condition-setting signals to still lower control systems. Each leg control system receives signals saying "forward, push, lean, lift..." (but not, of course, in words).

What's different about these reference conditions is that they can be frozen at a fixed setting and still remain the same reference condition. The soldier can halt with one foot in the air and hold that position, or halt standing on that foot, or halt with the leading and trailing foot both on the ground. The control systems are given varying reference conditions to create walking, but they are basically static control systems; they can hold a perception at a steady level.

These control systems don't send commands to the muscles, either. They set reference conditions for control systems that used to be called "spinal reflexes." Each signal from the higher static control system enters a little control system in the spinal cord telling it how much muscle length to sense (closely related to joint angle), and the muscle length system tells the lowliest control systems of all how much force to feel, using sensors that are embedded in the tendons attaching the muscles to the bones.

Nobody knows how many levels of control are really involved between maintaining a particular program in effect and maintaining a particular sensed muscle force matching a reference force. I have described only some of the stages suspected to exist between the control of programs and the control of muscle tensions. I have also described only levels *below* the program level; there are probably a couple of higher levels, at least a couple. If you decide that PCT is interesting enough for further study, there are some conjectures about the levels that you may want to read about in other books and papers. There is a summary of the levels I think may exist in the Reference section of this book.

The point here has been to sketch how a hierarchy of control might work. At each level of control there are control systems that specialize in controlling a particular type of perception; a program, or a sequence, or a static configuration, or a sensation. As we've seen it so far, it doesn't look much different from the idea of a command hierarchy, which many scientists have proposed before. *But a control hierarchy is not a command hierarchy.*

The difference is in what is commanded by a higher system. In a *command* hierarchy, the command specifies an action, an output. But in a *control* hierarchy, a command is a reference signal that specifies the state in which a particular perception is to be. A sequence controlling system does not tell the limbs to be in a particular configuration; it tells a control system at a lower level to *perceive* the limbs as being in a particular position, then another, then another. This little difference becomes important, indeed crucial, when we consider the subject of disturbances.

Suppose that the command (in the old way of thinking) is issued to make a leg move forward. Once this command is given, it is translated into muscle forces appropriate to that command. But suppose one's foot happens to have landed in a sticky mud-puddle. If the same muscle forces were generated that this command usually generates, there wouldn't be enough muscle force to pull the foot out of the mud; the usual muscle force is only enough to lift the leg under normal conditions.

So we would expect the person walking to pitch forward onto his, her, or its face.

However, this disturbance does *not* normally have that effect. What happens instead is that the leg muscles are instantly given a command to exert larger forces, and the foot is pulled free with almost no disturbance of the walking movement. In control-system terms, the stickiness of the mud momentarily made the sensed position of the leg lag behind the changing reference condition being set by higher systems. This led to an abnormally large error, which was translated immediately into a large change in the reference conditions for forces to be sensed by lower systems, and within a quite small fraction of a second the foot was pulled free and the sensed position of the leg caught up to the reference condition.

Notice that the reference condition for leg position didn't have to be adjusted at all to compensate for the disturbance. The control system receiving that reference condition took care of the effects of the sticky mud all by itself, by adjusting the reference conditions of lower-level systems. Because those are lower-level systems, they involve shorter neural pathways and simpler neural information processing; they are much faster than higher systems can be. Whereas a higher system might require half a second to perceive that a program is not progressing correctly and longer to start doing something about it, a lower system could start pulling the foot out of the mud in one-sixth of a second, plenty fast to prevent a disaster.

This can't happen in a top-down command-driven system. By the time the highest center in the brain that formulates the command can be informed that something has gone awry, it is too late. You're on your face in the mud, the car is off the road, or your drink is spilled all over the person you were hoping to impress.

In a control hierarchy, systems at each level are continuously monitoring the perceptions appropriate to that level and comparing them with reference conditions set by higher slower systems. If a disturbance occurs that changes a perception at some low level, the control system at that level immediately responds by altering the reference conditions closer to the lowest level, so the reaction to the disturbance produces a countering action as quickly as possible, without waiting for higher systems to recognize the problem. People have always understood that these "reflex" actions are much faster than thought-out, planned actions.

In a control system hierarchy, we combine the best features of the ideas of purely reflex action and cognitive planning. The higher systems, rather than telling the lower ones *how to act*, tell the lower systems *what to perceive*. It is up to the lower systems to produce whatever actions are required to make the real perception match the reference perception. This means that the higher systems don't have to plan what to do in case of disturbances; if the lower systems can take care of the disturbances, they will do so without being told. On the other hand, the higher systems can *change* the reference conditions for the lower systems, so unlike a reflex system, the lower systems can show different behaviors under the same circumstances. The car driver resisting deviations of the path of the car through "reflexive reactions" to the buffeting of crosswinds can also turn the wheel and *cause* the car to deviate from the straight line, for example to pass another car or take an off-ramp. A higher level in the driver can say "now drive straight" and "now drive in a curve." So the apparent reflex changes the way it reacts to external disturbances. The lower control systems (which is what reflexes actually are) can handle disturbances like crosswinds and bumps in the road without any higher-level direction; only the higher-level system, however, can handle the disturbance caused by a detour sign.

The most interesting and promising aspect of this idea of hierarchical control is that we can actually see it happening in other people without having to take a brain apart. This is mostly because we perceive the world pretty much as other people do, at least in the simpler ways, and can recognize when some aspect of the world is under control. Also, because of our own life experiences, we can often imagine what we would be experiencing if we were behaving the way someone else is behaving. This sort of projection of our own experiences onto others has to be done cautiously, of course, because people are far from *identical.* But we can often get a good idea of what is being controlled.

When we look at the marching soldiers doing a "column right," we can understand the program that is running in each soldier's head. At the same time, we can see other levels of control. We can see when one soldier has set a different reference condition for the sequences to be controlled; he's out of step or skipping instead of walking normally. We can see the soldiers maintaining a constant distance behind the person ahead, and away from the soldier to the left and right. We can see a soldier stumble over a stone and quickly get back into cadence. We can see all the soldiers lean a little when a strong gust of wind comes by. They lean, of course, *into* the wind. We can see that they are all maintaining their balance. When one soldier, daydreaming, turns the wrong way at the corner, we can see the rapid adjustments of lower-level reference conditions as he catches himself, spins around, runs to catch up, and fits himself into his place again, in step, all the while keeping his balance and moving himself perfectly competently.

What all this means is that if we can get the various levels of control sorted out properly, we can do experiments with them and understand how they work together. We can understand *why* a perception at one level is controlled by understanding *how* a perception at a higher level is controlled. We can see how perceptions at higher levels are derived from sets of perceptions at lower levels. Vast vistas of research topics open up; we can see how to build a theory of behavior that goes far beyond anything that the simpler concepts of cognitive planning of action or reflexive responses to stimuli could achieve. There are many scientists right now standing around scratching their heads and trying to see what to do next in exploring this rich new territory, like kids in a candy store.

Informal applications of this new idea of Hierarchical Perceptual Control Theory, or HPCT, are probably more evident right now than are any formal scientific applications. We're looking at a new paradigm for all the life sciences, probably the first new idea in a long while that really deserves to be called a paradigm in the late Thomas Kuhn's sense. In the rest of this book we'll be looking at some of the informal applications, as well as having a peek at some of the more formal ones that have been worked out. My main purpose, however, will remain that of giving you a solid feeling for this new theory, so you can start trying it on as a way of looking at behavior—the behavior of others and your own. With the science that is based on these new principles just getting under way, non-scientists have a pretty good chance of seeing things about this theory that others haven't come across yet, particularly in the area of seeing new interpretations of behaviors that have been taken for granted as already being explained. You, my esteemed, intelligent, and curious reader, are warmly invited to put a shoulder to the cart to help get it moving.

Chapter 4

Learning

In which learning is represented as a way of controlling the things that matter the most to us.

Learning

We've seen now that behavior involves control, which involves a circle of causation. We've seen how control can occur at many levels, each level manipulating the reference conditions that lower-level systems are unceasingly trying to match with perceptions by acting on the world outside them (which includes all lower-level systems). By now, you must be itching to ask some questions that start with "But." I can't guarantee that all those itches will be scratched, but we're going to tackle a question now that may help explain how the system got the way it is, and why. We're going to extend the theory to include a new kind of control system: one that acts on the organization of behavior instead of the outside world.

Consider a crying baby. Why is the baby crying? Some standard answers are because it is hungry, because it is thirsty, because it is sick, because a diaper pin is sticking into it, because it wants its mother, because it needs burping, because it needs changing, or simply because it can. All of these answers are reasonable, and all of them are also, I think, wrong.

The main thing I see wrong in these answers is that they are all given in terms that an adult observer, but not a baby, would understand. The right answer, I think, is that the baby cries because something is wrong. When everything is right, the baby does whatever contented babies do. When something is not right, the baby has only one means of control available: a whole-body effort in which the eyes are squeezed shut, tears are squeezed out of tear-ducts, the muscles squeeze the limbs into rigidity, and the diaphragm squeezes the air in the lungs through the vocal cords which are squeezed tight, creating a sound which on a slowed-down tape recording sounds like a grown man in terminal agony, and to a parent in real time sounds like a baby in trouble. All that makes this control system work is the fact that there is a caretaker standing by, one who does not like to see a baby in evident distress.

It's obvious why it is necessary for the baby to be under observation by a caretaker, and how this whole-body effort will inform the caretaker, by ceasing, when the right move has been made. The baby-caretaker interaction is interesting in its own right, but that isn't the path we will follow here. The question that the control theorist must consider first is: What do we mean by saying that the baby reacts to something that is "wrong"?

Babies have to breathe, eat, drink, stay warm, stay healthy, and be free of physical injury if they are to survive. If we went into the physiology and biochemistry of life, we would find that these are only superficial ways of describing the status of the life support systems in the baby. By the time the baby is born, a great many physiological and biochemical control systems are in working order, maintaining the internal state of the body in a viable condition. There is a hierarchy of control that extends downward from the organ systems, the hormone systems, and the cellular systems to the most detailed workings of the living organism—all the way, in fact, to the level of DNA, where enzymes created by the codes in the genetic materials move along the backbone of the long DNA molecules, repairing defects in those same codes, the most basic of all closed loops of causation.

When the baby is born, its primary occupation for the next few years will be to develop a hierarchy of behavioral control systems. These behavioral systems will work by operating the muscles, which will move the limbs, create facial expressions, make sounds, and in general produce physical consequences that affect things and people in the environment. But most important, these consequences of muscle actions will have strong effects on the baby itself, influencing how and when it will breathe, eat, drink, avoid pain, be cured of illness, and in general maintain its own life support systems. The problem is how the baby can learn behaviors that will in fact meet its real physiological and biochemical needs.

At the focus of this process of learning are the basic needs that have to be met. We need a theoretical link between those basic needs and the process of learning. Control theory suggests a link that is really a control system of a basic kind.

The object of control by this basic system is to keep certain physiological and biochemical variables near particular values: body temperature near 98+ degrees Fahrenheit, blood glucose, blood CO_2, and blood electrolytes at certain levels, and so forth. Whatever the list of critical variables may be, for each variable there is a particular state that represents an acceptable working level. What we need, then, is a set of reference conditions defined by inherited features of the system—perhaps simply thresholds of neural conduction or chemical reaction, or actual signals generated by built-in signal generators. We need a set of sensors that can report the actual state of each critical variable, and we need some comparison process that will create error signals when the sensed value of a critical variable differs from its reference condition.

This set of error signals gives us a model of what we mean by saying that the baby experiences something as "wrong." It isn't enough, for example, to note that the body temperature is 95 degrees F. By itself, that implies nothing except to a doctor—an external observer. Nor is it enough to state that the proper temperature is 98+ degrees. That bit of knowledge does nobody any good by itself. What we must have is a function inside the baby (rather than in the baby's doctor) that can compare the actual temperature with some representation of the right temperature, and generate a signal that represents the amount and direction of error. Only when this error is explicitly represented as a physical signal, a "wrongness signal," can the fact that the body temperature is lower than the right temperature lead to any physical actions, like shivering. And only then could we say that there is a basis for the baby's perceiving that something is wrong.

Obviously, not every variable involved in the body's life support systems can be involved in this wrongness-detection. Some processes are buried deep in the details of organ function and cellular function. For control of most of the variables in the physiological-biochemical systems, we rely entirely on the inherited systems to work right. It's only at the top level of physiological functioning that we can expect sensing of the general status of the life-support system to occur. We can sense a general release of adrenaline into the body and its immediate effects on physical sensations. We can detect a general lack of nutrition, a general temperature that is too low or too high, a general feeling of nausea or weirdness that goes with disease. We can recognize the feeling that arises when we haven't taken a breath recently enough; we know when something hurts. This is the level where the wrongness signals are generated, the signals that can serve as a basis for learning.

These wrongness signals are called, in PCT, "intrinsic error signals" because they refer to basic physical conditions that are essential for survival and are inside, intrinsic to, the body. We don't need to know how many of them exist or what conditions might be represented; that's a matter for many years of research to determine. All that matters now is that such a set of signals must exist, and that when some or many of these error signals are not zero, the body is equipped to do something that will restore them to zero. When the intrinsic error signals are restored to zero, all the associated critical variables are once again near their built-in reference states and the body should then be functioning normally, or as normally as can be defined by a limited set of signals. I took this idea, incidentally, from the cyberneticist W. Ross Ashby because I thought he was right, though I couldn't prove it.

All that remains is to turn the set of intrinsic error signals into learning. And here we run into a wall, not because we can't think of ways to do this, but because there are many ways and we have no data that will tell us which of these ways the human system actually uses—or whether it uses some method nobody has thought of.

There are many questions here that remain to be settled. Since we have no final answers now, we have to find some general way of completing this model of learning that doesn't commit us to any particular method, but that would remain generally applicable no matter what the facts turn out to be.

What we will do is to introduce an ordinary term used in a special way, "reorganization." Reorganization is a blanket term that means changing the way the nervous system is internally connected. Initially, when the baby is hungry or in pain, its nervous system is connected so it generates that whole-body effort of which crying is one of the side-effects. Considerably later, the same nervous system will be connected so that the child says "I'm hungry" or "I hurt" as one way of making the hunger or the hurt go away. This way of talking about reorganization leaves room for just about any specific theory of nervous-system learning that has been offered or will be offered. At the level of this discussion, that's all we need.

We now have a very basic control system concerned with keeping some set of critical variables near built-in reference conditions. As usual, this control system employs perception and comparison with reference conditions to generate an error signal that drives action. The action is left somewhat indefinite; it is the process of reorganization that alters the connections in the nervous system. We can refer to this control system as the "reorganizing system." This is the system that makes an adult human being out of a baby. It may actually consist of a lot of specialized reorganizing systems, but there's no point, considering how little we know, in getting into such details.

The most important aspect of the reorganizing system is that it is concerned *only* with maintaining intrinsic error signals as close to zero as possible. Its action consists of reorganizing the nervous system, which of course alters the way the person behaves in relation to the environment. But the *only* effect of this reorganizing process that matters to the reorganizing system is the effect on intrinsic error signals. Reorganizing—learning—continues as long as there is significant intrinsic error. It stops when, as a side-effect of the behavior that is learned, intrinsic error goes to zero. This process is not intelligent; it is simple and mechanical. It can't be intelligent because it has to work even in a tiny infant or even a fetus, long before complex intelligence arises in the brain.

The reorganizing system doesn't stop altering behavioral organization when something useful, reasonable, wise, or socially responsible is learned. It stops when intrinsic error goes to zero. So if the person wanders into some strange environment where the only way to get food is to put a rubber chicken into a bag and wave the bag overhead while yelling "Kalamazoo!"—the person will go on reorganizing until the behaving control systems find this a perfectly reasonable and necessary thing to do, so they get the food necessary to reduce the intrinsic error signal representing hunger to zero— unless the person dies of starvation first. And if these actions actually keep the person fed, the person will go on doing them because as long as the intrinsic error continues to be zero, there won't be anything to cause reorganization, and the present organization will just go on working the way it does. The point is not that we learn bizarre things because usually what we learn is ordinary and reasonable (or so it seems!). It is that learning is a fundamental and overriding process of change that continues as long as our inherited requirements for survival are not met, and that ceases or becomes much slower when they are met. There may be other modes of learning, but reorganization is the basic mode.

This concept of error-driven reorganization is a distinct departure from traditional notions of the causes of learning. The main traditional notion is that of "reinforcement." The idea is that the person starts by behaving more or less randomly, emitting all sorts of behaviors that have all sorts of effects. When one of those effects happens to be of a kind that is "reinforcing," the behavior that caused it is made (by some unspecified means) a little more likely to occur again. As this process goes on and on, the reinforcing effect occurs more often, making the behavior that produced it ever more likely to occur, until finally that behavior occurs all the time and continuously produces the reinforcement. The continuing reinforcement maintains the behavior that is producing it.

The reorganization idea is essentially the reversed image of the idea of reinforcement. Under the reorganization concept, behavior continually changes as long as there is intrinsic error. When an effect of behavior is to reduce intrinsic error, the next change in organization is delayed, so that the behavior that happened to reduce intrinsic error persists a little longer. When the behavioral organization is found that reduces intrinsic error to zero (or whatever the required lower threshold is), the behavioral organization that then exists simply continues to operate unmodified.

So under reinforcement theory, a reinforcing effect of behavior has a positive effect on producing that same behavior, while under reorganization theory, a beneficial effect of behavior *reduces* the chances that the organization producing that behavior will be *altered* by further reorganization.

These two ideas sound very similar, but their implications are quite different. To make reinforcement theory work, we have to imagine that a reinforcer like a piece of candy has some inherent effect on organisms, an effect that increases the likelihood of the specific behavior that causes the reinforcer to appear. To explain why some consequences of behavior are reinforcing and some are not, we would have to guess what the reinforcers have in common—what physical properties they share. And to explain why a given kind of reinforcement can cause a specific behavior to be produced on one occasion but not another, we have to invent new phenomena just to take care of the failure of a reinforcer to work. If an animal finds 10 milligrams of salt in its food to be reinforcing, why is 1,000 milligrams not even more reinforcing? We have to say that 10 milligrams is reinforcing, but 1,000 milligrams causes "satiation."

The concept of reorganization accounts more compactly for all that the concept of reinforcement explains. The single concept of the reference condition explains both the seeking of rewarding things and satiation—it defines what is meant by "not enough,"

"enough," and "too much." Reorganization theory also explains some things that reinforcement theory has never been able to explain. For example, why is it that in order to make an animal behave in a certain way by reinforcing it with food, we must first starve the animal, and then make sure that the animal can't find food on its own? And why is it that to make food a reinforcer, we can't just deprive the animal of water? Reinforcement theory is an attempt to account for behavior strictly in terms of external observations, with no (obvious) model of the organism being used. That means, by the rules of this theory, that we can't say that the animal is reinforced by food because it is hungry. We can't observe hunger from outside the animal.

Reorganization theory relies on a model of the internal workings of the organism. It says that we learn in order to satisfy internal needs, and that we stop varying the way we behave in a given environment (although we don't stop behaving) when those needs are met. It explains why being deprived of food means that we will not stop learning until what we have learned specifically provides food for ourselves and continues to do so. It shows why nothing is reinforcing unless we lack it, and of course need or want it. Anything that causes intrinsic error makes changes of organization start; anything that terminates intrinsic error stops them.

There's one more basic difference between reorganization theory and reinforcement theory. When we learn something, just what is it that we learn? According to reinforcement theory, we learn to produce specific actions—"responses"—when specific "discriminative stimuli" occur. But according to reorganization theory, what we learn is *a control system*. As we saw in previous chapters, a control system varies its actions in order to keep some perception under control. The particular action produced depends on what disturbances are acting at the same time as well as on the current setting of the reference condition. In keeping the car centered in its lane, we might twist the wheel rightward at one time, and then, to keep the car in exactly the same position, twist it leftward at another time. When we learn to drive, we don't learn steering wheel movements; we learn to control a *relationship* between deviations of the car from where we want to see it and the effort we apply to the steering wheel. This is very different from learning that when a certain stimulus occurs, we should emit a certain response.

There are other kinds of learning beside reorganization. Learning someone's e-mail address is primarily a matter of remembering it or writing it down. Learning the outcome of a mystery is simply a matter of reading the book to the end. The word "learning" is used in many contexts where the idea of reorganization would be overkill. Rather than trying to revise everyone's languages, the best approach is just to say "reorganization" when we mean acquiring a new control skill as a way of satisfying intrinsic needs, and to use "learning" only when we intend to be vague.

It's possible that as the brain's organization becomes more complex, it learns methods of learning. That's an interesting possibility, but it doesn't help us answer the basic question of how learning gets started. The brain must acquire the ability to carry out complex strategies before learning-to-learn can happen. The concept of error-driven reorganization accounts for the way learning begins, and probably for the way basic kinds of learning continue throughout life. It will carry us a long way toward a usable theory of behavior.

Chapter 5

Hands-On PCT

*In which we play some games
to experiment with
real control behavior*

Hands-On PCT

We now have a fairly broad view of PCT, Perceptual Control Theory, that includes control of particular perceptions and a hierarchical system for controlling some perceptions as a means of controlling others. We have at least a rudimentary theory of reorganization that shows how the hierarchy of control might develop, and how its development relates to maintaining the well-being of the person. As far as I've been able, I've tried to base the theoretical aspects of this discussion on everyday experience, on facts about behavior that are accessible to anyone. But reading and experiencing are not the same; it's time we indulge in a little recreation and look into learning through doing.

There's a little game with endless variations that illustrates many of the basic principles of PCT. The equipment required is very simple: two people and two rubber bands. You can ask a neurosurgeon to sever your corpus callosum and split your brain into two independent personalities, and play this game with yourself, but I recommend that you find a friend and do it the easy way. The point of this game is to get some experience with (a) consciously observing yourself controlling, and (b) observing how you can interact with another person who is controlling. As you play the rubber-band game you will see all the basic principles at work, and get an understanding of them that words alone can't convey. After you've seen the basic idea, we'll go on to introduce the first important application of PCT to human problems, the problem of conflict.

To set up the game, you first knot the two rubber bands together by passing each through the other and pulling them tight. This will produce something like an elongated figure-8 with a knot at the crossing point. Each rubber band should be about 3 or 4 inches long when relaxed. For the initial experiment, you should use rubber bands from the same batch, as identical as reasonably possible.

It will help to have a sheet of paper, 8½ by 11, that you can lay on a table between you and your partner (seated across from each other or next to each other). Put a small round black dot in the middle of the paper. Each person now hooks one finger through an end of the rubber bands, so the rubber bands are stretched horizontally about an inch or less above the paper. If you're side-by-side, use the outboard hands to hold the rubber bands, to avoid bumping into each other.

Designate one person as E and the other as C: Experimenter and Controller. The roles can be swapped periodically to give both people the opportunity to see what's going on from both viewpoints.

The task of the controller is very simple: Keep the knot joining the rubber bands exactly over the dot on the piece of paper. The more accurately C can do this, the clearer will be the principles being illustrated. The reference condition that C adopts is "knot over dot." Of course the reference condition is not those words; it's the perceptual situation that we describe by using those words.

The experimenter E uses E's end of the rubber bands to disturb the position of the knot in the horizontal plane. E can do this by pulling away from the knot or moving toward it, or moving at right angles to the line of the rubber bands, or any combination of these moves. The most important thing for E to understand is that the object of this experiment is *not* to prevent C from controlling the position of the knot. If E yanks violently at the rubber band or uses a series of rapid movements and jerks, C won't be able to carry out the task very well and the basic phenomenon will be obscured by the extreme disturbances. So whatever moves E makes, they should be smooth and not too fast. Of course after the basic observations are made, E can try all sorts of things to see what control looks like under difficult conditions. But basically, we want to keep the conditions easy.

Start with a little practice, so C can learn to get good control of the knot (I use the vague term "learn" because I don't know whether true reorganization or some other method of acquiring a new skill is involved). E moves the disturbing end of the rubber bands around in any kind of slow patterns, while C concentrates on accurately keeping the knot over the dot. A few minutes' practice should be enough.

The first relationship that will strike you is the one between E's hand and C's hand. Everything E does, C does. If E pulls back, C pulls back. If E moves clockwise around the dot, C moves clockwise. Discounting small control errors, at every moment C's hand is exactly as far from the dot as E's hand (assuming the rubber bands are identical), and the line from E's end to C's end passes through the dot.

If a third observer happened on this scene, what would the

first impression of these actions be? It would be that C is mirroring the movements of E symmetrically around the dot. It wouldn't be obvious which person is putting in the disturbances and which one is counteracting them. Even if E confessed to being the disturber, it would still not be obvious that control is happening. Much more likely, the third observer would see E doing things and C reacting to them: stimulus and response.

This is a reasonable interpretation based only on a quick judgment. The third observer might well lose interest at that point, and leave with the impression that this control theory stuff is just the same old stimulus and response idea that's been around since great-grandpa. But a swift glance is not enough to reveal that control is going on.

Remember the basic organization proposed by PCT: perception, comparison of the perception with a reference condition, detection of error, and conversion of error into an action that affects the perception. Perception, comparison, action. According to this theory, C is perceiving the position of the knot relative to the dot as it actually is at any moment. The perceived relationship is compared with a reference condition, knot over dot. The difference, the perceived distance of the knot from the dot at any time, is converted into an action, a motion of C's end of the rubber bands, that will bring the perception of the knot-to-dot distance to the reference state, zero distance (that is what knot-over-dot means: no distance between knot and dot).

How could we test to see if this model is right, or if the stimulus-response interpretation is just as good? According to PCT, what is being controlled is a perception of the knot and dot. The stimulus-response interpretation (in one form) says that C is responding to movements of E's hand. So the two theories are actually claiming that C is responding to different perceptions of the situation, and we ought to be able to decide which claim is right.

An easy test would be to get a piece of cardboard and use it to keep C from seeing first E's hand, and then the position of the knot. If C has been responding to movements of E's hand, then blocking the view of E's hand while still allowing the knot to be seen should at least greatly modify C's behavior. On the other hand, if C is perceiving the relationship of knot to dot, blocking the view of E's hand should have no effect on C's actions, while blocking the view of the knot and dot should at least make control much worse, if not destroy it. If you're feeling the need for a formal proof you can actually try this. A much easier approach is simply asking C, "Are you watching E's hand or the knot?" C will deny paying attention to E's hand. And if you actually do the test, you will see that blocking the view of E's hand and everything on that side clear up to (but not including) the knot has no effect at all on C's behavior or on the accuracy of control of the knot, while blocking the view of the knot drastically reduces the accuracy of control. Of course C can switch to perceiving and controlling the symmetry of the hand positions, but this will not accomplish the perfect mirroring that we saw before.

Doing this test even more formally, using instrumentation and computers, shows that control of the knot-to-dot distance depends critically on the controller's being able to see the knot and the dot, and not at all on the ability to see the cause of disturbances of the knot.

You can put the rubber bands down for a moment. PCT researchers have done many variations on this sort of experiment using calibrated handles and computer displays where the variables can be measured 60 times per second with an accuracy of 1 part in 1,000 or better. In addition to the test just mentioned, many other non-PCT hypotheses have been tested. One of them is simply that the stimulus is the movement of the knot, and the response is the movement of C's hand. Now the interesting fact about the movements of the knot (or whatever variable is being controlled) is that these movements are very small if the controller is skilled. Small movements of the knot lead to large movements of the hand because the disturbances used can become quite large but the knot movements remain small. One quick way to test the idea that the hand position depends on the perception of the knot position is to calculate the statistical correlation between knot position and hand position. The result is quite surprising: The correlation is usually less than 0.1 and can even be negative. For non-fans of statistics, that means that there is essentially no relationship between the knot movements and the hand movements. A simple stimulus-response explanation that does not take the closed loop into account fares very poorly as a way of predicting behavior.

This lack of a correlation between an apparent cause and its apparent effect is absurd, of course, but it is a fact. A more detailed analysis shows that the low correlation is caused by small random variations in the behavior ("system noise"), which are comparable to the position errors that the control system is trying to reduce. Random variations in the knot position that represent system noise naturally don't correlate with the hand positions. What human control systems can do, apparently, is to keep the errors so small that system noise predominates. No control system can do better than this.

That was a bone thrown to readers who like a bit of technical crunch to go with the main course. You can pick up the rubber bands again.

There's another angle to testing for control. Let C, for a moment, hold C's end of the rubber bands stationary. Let E start with the rubber bands almost slack, and then pull directly away from the dot by about six inches. Watch the knot. The knot will move half as far as E's end of the rubber bands moves. This shows us the effect on the knot that E's disturbance would have if C did nothing. E could, just by examining the rubber bands, figure out that this is what would happen. If C went to lunch, E could stick a pin in the table to hold C's end in one position, and experimentally determine how disturbances would affect the knot with no control system present.

When C comes back, E can now apply exactly the same disturbance as before, and observe what the knot does. Now, of course, pulling back by a calibrated amount will have essentially no effect on the position of the knot. The knot will move only a tiny fraction of the amount that it moved when there was no control system attached to the other end. This *failure* of the disturbance *to have the physically predicted effect* is a strong clue that there is a control system acting. It's not infallible as a proof that control exists because you still have to rule out simpler explanations for the lack of effect, but it's infallible in the other direction. If the amount of movement of the knot is exactly what you would predict under the assumption that there is no control system, then you have ruled out the existence of a control system. This test can eliminate wrong guesses very quickly, which is almost as helpful as being told what the right guess would be.

As I said, this rubber-band experiment has many interesting variations. Here's one that you can skip if you aren't turned on by subtle effects. Use a marking pen to put a dot on both rubber bands about an inch from the knot. C now can choose which mark to keep over the dot. E is to use the formal test just described to decide which mark C is controlling. This involves predicting how much each mark would move if C did nothing, and then, with C controlling, seeing which mark is ruled out as being controlled. In this simple situation the answer is easy, but perhaps you can see how this test, in more complex situations, could be used to track down non-obvious controlled perceptions by eliminating all but one reasonable possibility.

So far C has been acting like a one-level control system. Let's make it two, and kill two birds with one stone. This time, C, make the knot move very slowly and uniformly around the dot in a small circle, with a radius of about one inch. By "slowly" I mean that the knot should take at least ten seconds to go once around the circle. E, of course, continues to move the other end of the rubber bands in big smooth slow random patterns. If E sees that C is having trouble, slow down the disturbances. We want to see the controller succeeding, not failing.

The first bird bites the dust when you see that the reference condition is no longer "knot on dot." Perhaps, like many theoreticians in this field have done, you unconsciously assumed that the dot was specifying the reference condition. The knot was the controlled perception, and it was brought to the reference condition set by the dot. That, of course, changes the person into a comparator, or puts the comparison process into the environment. Very confusing.

Now, however, we can see that the controlled variable was really the relationship between the knot and the dot, and we just happened to pick a reference-relationship that required the knot and the dot to be in the same position. Now that's no longer true; the knot is being maintained in an ever-changing relationship to the dot. And if you still think the dot is not simply part of the controlled perception, we can let E choose to move the piece of paper as well as the rubber band. C is controlling a relationship between two perceptions, one of the dot and the other of the knot, and keeping this relationship in a match with a reference relationship that now involves continuous motion.

If you're just reading this description, this won't be obvious, but if you're at the stage of doing the experiment you will realize that the experimenter, all this time, has been moving the disturbing end of the rubber bands around in big continuous patterns. You may have been thinking that to make the knot move in a circle, C has to make the hand holding the rubber band move around in a bigger circle. But if C held a marking pen through the loop in the rubber band so a record of hand movements would be left on the paper (this is worth trying), the trace would show not circular movements but a random mess. This is the second dead bird.

In the movements of the knot relative to the dot, we are seeing the reference condition that C has established. The reference condition determines what the controlled perception will do. But in the movements of the hand, we see a composite of the effect of the reference condition and an even larger effect of the ongoing disturbances. The hand movements don't correspond either to the reference condition or to the disturbance; they represent what has to be done to maintain control when the disturbance is changing.

Let C now stop the motion of the knot at a point one inch to the left of the dot (E keeps on applying disturbances). Now we are back to the original case, where C's hand movements are symmetrical with those of E—but the knot is being maintained in a different and now stationary relationship to the dot. The control process is just like the one we started with, but with a different reference condition. We can call this one level of control.

The second level of control perceives in terms of *continuous change*. When the reference condition for this kind of change is "one revolution every 10 seconds," or the perceptual equivalent of that statement, the knot moves in a circle because the reference relationship for knot position is being changed so as to maintain that perceived circular movement. The first level of control, which is concerned with maintaining a particular relative position of the knot and dot, is being used as the output of the second level of control, which is being used to maintain a perception of circular movement. The position control system is being used as part of a motion or trajectory control system. C could use a different trajectory control system, and make the knot write C's name. Many different higher-level control processes could be carried out using this same position-control system (although not at the same time). You may (I hope) remember Chapter 3, where the idea of a hierarchy of control systems was brought up. We're seeing an example of it here.

Many more variations are possible, involving multiple rubber bands, more than two people, and simultaneous control of more than one perception. They're fun to explore, but we have to be moving on.

There's one last demonstration that will carry us into the next chapter. On the piece of paper, add a second dot about $1/4$ inch to one side of the dot that's already there. Now E disappears and becomes another controller, C2; we have C1 and C2 both controlling the same knot.

The experiment is very simple. C1 holds the knot exactly over the old dot, and C2 holds it exactly over the new dot. The two controllers might seem to be cooperating in controlling the knot—but their ideas of the reference condition differ by $1/4$ inch.

If both controllers insist on keeping the knot over the "right" dot, there's only one possible outcome. A rubber band will break.

This innocent situation exemplifies the most serious problem that can arise between control systems, whether they are in different people or inside one person. It's called conflict, and PCT explains exactly how conflict works and how it can cause immense difficulties. This subject is worth a chapter or two.

I do hope that you will actually try the rubber-band game. It provides insights that you will never get by trying to imagine what these words mean. Control is a real phenomenon, an unmistakable phenomenon, an understandable phenomenon. The theory we call PCT makes sense of it both as we see it in another person and as we experience it ourselves. Playing with rubber bands may seem childish and undignified for a grown person, but it is no more childish than rolling little balls down a slanted piece of wood was for Galileo.

Chapter 6

Inner Conflict

*In which we see what happens
when control systems
inside one person come into
conflict with each other*

Inner Conflict

As we've just seen in the rubber band demo, a conflict can arise when two control systems attempt to control the same thing, but relative to two different reference levels. If one person succeeds in getting the knot over Dot 1, the other person necessarily can't be seeing the knot over Dot 2. So the other person will try harder, dragging the knot toward Dot 2—which will, of course, drag it off of Dot 1, so the first person will also try harder. As this goes on, the rubber bands get longer and longer, eventually breaking.

Actually, I have seen the rubber band break only once, and that was because *both* people decided that they didn't care if it broke. Generally, at least one person will not want to break the rubber bands, and so will limit how hard he or she will pull. That person doesn't want a hand hurt when the rubber band breaks and snaps back, or just feels it would be wrong or wasteful to break the equipment.

This is a conflict between two people, but we will focus here on the conflict within one of the people, the one who wants the rubber band to remain whole, for whatever reason. This person has a dilemma: In order to keep the knot over the right dot, it is necessary to pull hard enough to keep it there. But as the other person continues to pull harder, "hard enough" gets close to "hard enough to break the rubber band." At that point the reference signal that says "no broken rubber band" comes into play, and the person becomes reluctant to pull any harder.

So now this person finds that the same "pulling on the rubber band" control system is being given two exactly opposite goals: Pull harder, and don't pull harder (or pull less hard). Pull harder because the knot is supposed to be exactly over the dot, and pull less hard because the rubber band should not break.

This is the essence of an internal conflict. A true internal conflict boils down to a clear impossibility: Accomplish this, and at the same time don't accomplish this, or accomplish the opposite.

There are always at least two levels of control involved in an internal conflict. One level is the place where the conflict is *expressed*: A single control system is being given two different reference conditions that must be satisfied at the same time. The second level consists of two control systems, the ones that are *creating* the conflict by setting these different reference conditions.

At the level where the conflict is expressed, we have two different reference signals entering the comparator function of a single control system. A comparator, in the PCT model, is a very simple thing: If it receives more than one reference signal they are simply added together to make one effective reference signal. If a positive and a negative reference signal are sent to the same comparator, the net reference signal is their sum. A reference signal of +10 units combined with a reference signal of -9 units in the same comparator is the same as a single reference signal of 1 unit.

So imagine that one reference signal says "pull with a force of 10 units" and the other says "pull with a force of -2 units." How hard will the "pull" control system actually pull? Eight units of pull, as sensed.

Now look at the level where the conflict is being created. The control system that wants to keep the knot over the dot needs to set a reference pull of +10 units in order to cancel the other person's pull. But it is getting a pull of only 8 units. The other control system, which has decided, say, that 6 units of pull would break the rubber bands has actually set a negative reference level for pull, trying to reduce the pull. But it is perceiving 8 units of pull.

What will happen? The system that wants the knot on the dot will increase the reference setting for the pull system, and the system that wants to keep the pull less than 6 units will specify an even more negative reference setting for the same system. And of course the actual reference pull will be somewhere between these settings, too small to satisfy one control system and too large to satisfy the other.

At the level where the conflict is *expressed*, the lower level, notice that this control system is working perfectly. If the net reference signal says "8 units of pull," that system adjusts the position of the hand holding the rubber band until the pull is sensed as exactly 8 units. Nothing wrong there!

But at the level where the conflict is *created*, nothing is right. The "knot over dot" control system needs 10 units of pull, or more, and isn't seeing the knot over the dot; the "don't break the rubber band" control system needs to sense less than 6 units of pull, and is sensing a lot more than that. The two control systems at the higher level are failing because of the conflict. The lowest-level system isn't doing what either of them wants, even though it is working perfectly.

I said that "at least two" levels are involved. Actually, that should be "at least three." To see what I mean, repeat the first simple experiment in which one person tries to keep the knot over one dot while another person varies the disturbance. You be the experimenter, and ask a friend to keep the knot over Dot 1, cautioning the friend please, please not to break the rubber bands. Then just keep pulling harder. At some point the conflict will appear: Just observe what happens next, as you keep pulling harder and harder.

First, as the friend starts to become fearful that the rubber band will break, control of the knot will start to deteriorate. And almost immediately, you will see your friend do something about the conflict. Most likely, your friend will start talking to you. "Hey, don't pull so hard, the rubber band is going to break!" If you just keep pulling harder, the most likely thing to happen next is that your friend will stop playing the game.

This is where the next level of control is seen. The goals of keeping the knot over the dot and of not breaking the rubber bands don't spring out of nowhere. They are being set and maintained by higher-level control systems—a minimum of one level higher, making at least three levels altogether involved in this conflict. These higher systems create the *situation* in which the conflict appears.

At least one aspect of the situation has to change in order to do away with the conflict. The reference condition "knot over dot" can be changed, or that whole control system can be abandoned. The reference condition "don't break the rubber bands" can be changed. Or the person can simply choose to put down the end of the rubber band and do something else, like discussing the experiment with you, ceasing to use *either* of the conflicting systems.

In these experiments, most people, in one way or another, will change the situation by ceasing to play the game. "That's very interesting, I see what you mean," they will say, relaxing their pull altogether. They will change the situation to one of talking about the experiment, or about their feelings while doing it, or something— something that is *not* simply enduring the conflict any longer. At that point they are no longer trying to keep the knot over the dot, or keep the rubber bands from breaking. The conflicting control systems have become unemployed.

So in any conflict, we can see three levels of organization: the lowest level where the conflict is *expressed*, the next level where the conflict is *caused*, and at least one higher level that is creating the *situation* that gives rise to the conflict. In the background, of course, are physical realities; the rubber bands will in fact break if subjected to a large enough pull, and given the disturbance that exists, a certain amount of pull is actually needed to keep the knot over the dot. But there are many such physical aspects to all of behavior, and few of the possible conflicts ever occur. What permits the conflict to occur is getting yourself into a *situation* where you have to satisfy two incompatible reference conditions at once. You can't change the physical realities, but you can change the situations you choose as reference conditions.

Resolving Inner Conflicts

One of the properties of a control system that makes it useful in behavior is that it can automatically resist disturbances, without higher systems having to tell it to do so. "Automatically" is the significant word here. Consciousness is normally involved in learning how to control something—think of a baby's total absorption in getting a hand into contact with a toy—but soon control becomes skilled and then automatic. Once control is automatic, all you have to do is think of the perception you want, and it is delivered without delay or fuss. By the time we are adults, most of our control processes are done this way, without need to pay attention to how they are accomplished. If you want to pick up a pencil, it immediately becomes picked up. You don't have to stop and think how to do it.

This is fine as long as you don't run into a conflict situation. When we first started doing the rubber-band experiment, there were no conflicts because it probably never occurred to anyone involved to pull hard enough to threaten the rubber bands. By the time most people have gone through the introductory series of experiments, they have learned to control the knot almost automatically. So when the second dot is added, many of them are lulled into thinking this is just another control demo, and they start—for a few seconds anyway—obediently keeping the knot over the assigned dot. Only it doesn't work.

The first thing that usually happens is that the controller's attention is brought sharply to a focus where the conflict is *expressed*. The hand refuses to pull any harder. The control process that was automatic now becomes fully conscious again. That paralyzed hand is a big problem.

Of course that's the wrong level; there's nothing wrong with the control system that moves the hand to create a certain amount of pull. The *hand* is not deciding not to pull harder. The pull control system is being given conflicting orders as to how much pull to perceive, and it's making the perceived pull follow the net result of the two reference conditions instead of one or the other of them.

Next, it becomes obvious to the conscious controller that the *real* problem is that the knot is away from the dot, and that the rubber band is too stretched for comfort. Attention goes to the *cause* of the conflict. And, quite often, that is where it stays. The person might try wiggling the knot so it is on the dot some of the time, thinking (erroneously) that the tension can be relieved fast enough to avoid breaking the rubber bands. In this situation there isn't much else that could be tried, so unless the person can see the problem at still a higher level, the conflict will just go on.

The real solution to the conflict occurs when the person realizes consciously that playing this game is impossible: The situation is such that the two reference conditions can't be achieved at the same time. What needs to be changed is the *desired situation*, so one or both of the conflicting reference conditions can be adjusted to eliminate the conflict. If the higher systems are not changed, you may reorganize the lower systems all you please, but the higher systems will adjust the reference signals until the conflict is in full force again. You gotta keep that knot over the dot, and you gotta keep those rubber bands from breaking—a physical impossibility, no matter which hand is used to hold the rubber band, or whether you squint or close your eyes.

Side-comment: I'm using the word "situation" as a blanket term for whatever higher-level reference conditions are involved. The actual names of the levels involved are unimportant in thinking about inner conflict; all that matters is the *relative* levels of the control systems.

There's one level where the conflict is expressed; a higher level at which it's caused, and a higher level still that is responsible for setting the incompatible reference conditions. Whether this triad of levels exists low in the nervous system or at the highest levels is irrelevant. The principle remains the same.

The rubber-band situation shows what's wrong with having inner conflicts. When there's no conflict, you can play the rubber-band game quite successfully, and use it to tell people about control theory, or learn about it. And when you're not playing that game, you can keep from breaking rubber bands without giving much thought to the subject. There are good reasons for playing the game, and presumably good reasons for not going around breaking rubber bands; you wouldn't want to lose the ability to achieve either of these ends.

But when the conflict situation arises, that is exactly what happens: *You lose the ability to do either of those things.* And who is responsible for this loss of control? Only you are. You are using each control system to keep the other one from successfully controlling. You might object, "Yes, but you were the one who got me into this situation!" The answer is obvious: I may be the one who got you into it, but you're the one who agreed to get into it, and who, unless you change your mind about something, is going to keep you in it. And if there's a way out of the conflict, you're the one who is going to have to find it.

Our first reaction to encountering a conflict is normally to start using our higher-order systems—using our noodles, as the saying goes—to fix the problem. We call on whatever we already know how to do as a way of solving it. A while back, I had our imaginary controller say "Hey, don't pull so hard, the rubber band is going to break!" This is an attempt to affect one of the *causes* of the conflict; if the disturbance could be made smaller, this person wouldn't have to pull so hard. But that doesn't actually resolve the problem because the potential for conflict is just as great as ever; you've simply removed one of the immediate causes, temporarily, assuming I pay any attention to the request, which if you will recall I didn't.

Sometimes it's possible to change one of the causes of a conflict without changing the situation. If so, that's what you do and you put off resolving the problem to another time when this doesn't work. But some people are smarter than that.

It often happens, in the demonstration using the two dots, that one or both parties will immediately see the impossibility of what's being asked of the participants. They see the impossibility right away, and refuse to play. There's a conflict between performing the demo to please me, and not performing the demo so as to avoid getting into a silly and obvious conflict, but evidently this conflict also gets resolved right away, with the result that the situation is simply not accepted. People who do this are happy to discuss the conflict situation as a hypothetical problem, but they're very reluctant actually to get into it. As I said, some people are smarter.

I usually persuade them to do it anyway because "hypothetical" isn't good enough. You have to *experience* this problem to understand how to analyze it. There is nothing so useful as actually seeing the theory working in a real situation. We're not talking about "hypothetical." We're talking about what really happens.

A lot of people will not say, "Hey, don't pull so hard, the rubber bands are going to break." They will say "...*You're* going to break the rubber bands." In a conflict situation it's easy to overlook the part your own automatic control systems are playing. If you weren't trying to keep the knot on the dot, there wouldn't be any problem, would there? When you focus on the cause of a conflict, the effects of your own goals tend to disappear from sight. "Hey, you're cheating!" you complain to a person who's beating you at chess. But if you were trying to lose, wouldn't that just help you get what you want? You complain to someone, "How I wish I could stop procrastinating!" But would you wish that if there were no desire to put things off?

When we try to cope with conflicts at the level where they're caused, we tend to take a one-sided view of the problem. You say to your happily chatting mother, "Mom, you're making me late for my date!" But if you didn't want to be talking to your mother, or at least listening to her (for whatever higher reasons), you wouldn't be hanging around, would you? Who is making you late for your date? She's pulling on that rubber band, but who's pulling on the other end?

In every conflict situation there are *two* things you want, not just one. You may consciously adopt one of them as what you "really" want, but you want the other one, too—it's just that right at the moment, you've forgotten why. So you feel that one of the wants is justified, while the other isn't.

In fact, both of the reference conditions for the opposing control systems are being set as parts of different higher-level control processes. They are both "justified," but in different contexts. This is why you can't resolve a conflict at the level where it's being caused. Somehow you have to focus your attention on the level that is creating the situation in which the conflict arises. So we have to try to get a handle on the "somehow."

A Reasonable Hypothesis

Remember Chapter 4, on learning? In that chapter I introduced an idea called "reorganization," which is a basic mode of learning. When you're trying to resolve a conflict, and nothing you already know how to do works, the only resource you have left is reorganization, which amounts to trying something new at random and seeing if things get better or worse. If they get worse, you reorganize again right away; otherwise you wait a while.

Unfortunately, reorganization as presented in Chapter 4 is basically an automatic random process, and it doesn't produce any specific new organization. It just comes up with whatever will correct intrinsic error—basically, it makes you feel better in some generalized sense. It's not very useful for solving any *specific* problem; there's simply no way to predict the outcome.

At the very least, it would be nice if reorganization could somehow be confined to whatever part of the brain is having control problems such as those caused by conflict. If you are having a conflict at a certain level, there's no point in reorganizing at a *lower* level, or in reorganizing a control system that's working perfectly well. But how could the reorganizing effects be directed to the systems that need reorganizing, without affecting those that don't? This isn't your problem, of course; it's mine as the theoretician who is proposing a model. So what story can I come up with that doesn't seem completely far-fetched, and has even a modicum of evidence in favor of it?

There are really two problems: Why should a conflict lead to reorganization, and how does reorganization get directed to the right place?

The first problem is relatively easy to handle. Anywhere in the hierarchy, any control system that is working properly will be keeping its own error signal small, most of the time. So we can simply add "error signals at any level in the hierarchy" to the list of proposed intrinsic error signals. The inherited reference level for error signals in the hierarchy, treated as intrinsic variables, is zero. When error signals become large enough for long enough, the reorganizing system wakes up and starts to alter connections in the brain. (Naturally this could be done by a lot of little localized reorganizing systems, but we don't need that level of detail.) Conflicts can result in big error signals; therefore they can start reorganization going.

The second problem, of getting reorganization to work in the right place, might seem to be solved by the idea of little localized reorganization systems, but that isn't sufficient as a general answer. The loss of control that comes with conflict will, to be sure, result in large error signals. But it will also have effects of other kinds, indirectly resulting from the loss of control. Even more important, there are spurious solutions to conflict, such as simply avoiding situations where it might arise, that do not lead to large error signals in the hierarchy, but which nevertheless can have bad effects. Maybe the situation you're avoiding is one that you need to be in frequently in order, for example, to get food. Lack of food can be a long way removed from the actual reasons you don't like to eat in front of other people. Somehow, reorganization has to be directed not to the eating systems, but to the systems that are concerned with social relationships or self-concepts. Little localized reorganizing systems aren't going to help with that sort of situation.

While we can't rule out localized reorganizing systems, there is a fairly convincing hypothesis that would seem to fit certain observations and that would fit the way we seem to resolve inner conflicts in many situations. It is this: Reorganization follows awareness (or consciousness). When we focus awareness on some limited part of the brain's operations, that is where reorganization is most likely to occur if there is a problem—a large error. That hypothesis can be taken further, but this is far enough for present purposes.

(I apologize for involving readers in a theoretician's musings, but perhaps some will find the line of reasoning interesting.)

Let's say that reorganization follows the focus of awareness or consciousness, or if you wish, attention. From here on, that's a fact, even if it may not remain a fact forever.

Now we can see why it is that focusing on the level where a conflict is *caused* will not resolve the conflict. You may reorganize how you pull on the rubber bands, from what position, with which hand or foot, as felt or seen, or accompanied by whatever other acts you end up producing, but the fact will remain that as long as the goal is to keep the knot on the dot at the same time the rubber bands are not overstressed, the same conflict will persist. It may not be manifested all the time, but it is lurking there ready to come into play as soon as the appropriate situation occurs. There is a bug in the system, *and it is not at this level of organization.*

The bug is in the higher-level systems that are setting these incompatible reference conditions. If reorganization really does follow attention, you have to shift your attention away from the immediate causes of the conflict to a higher level, the level that is creating the situation in which conflict occurs. You have to go up a level.

I could have said all that much more simply, but I'm uncomfortable with bringing tablets down off mountains and flinging them to the ground in front of people. If you understand where the inscriptions came from, you can make up your own mind whether you want to copy any of them for your own use.

Going Up a Level

I have invented a way of going up a level that seems to work quite well. The fact that this method has been invented before (approximately one million times) will not, I hope, weaken my claim to fame. It's actually a natural mechanism for resolving conflict, and it's been known under a wide variety of names, like insight, reflection, meditation (of several flavors), higher consciousness, and even "dissociation." The basic phenomenon that has been noticed again and again throughout history (alas for fame) is quite simple. The position in the structure of experience from which we consciously observe the world is movable.

This implies that the organization of the brain covers considerably more territory than we can encompass in awareness at one time. The whole brain is always working, but as conscious entities we participate in only part of its activities at a given moment.

Archimedes, it is said, while getting into a full bathtub, suddenly understood how to measure the volume of immersed objects, and focusing his attention entirely on this monumental discovery, ran naked and dripping through the streets shouting "I have found it!" If he had stubbed his bare toe and fallen, he probably would not have noticed. I don't know if his compatriots were shocked by his lack of modesty, but if they were, and if Archimedes were blushing, Archimedes would not have noticed that, either. To Archimedes the conscious man, the whole world had shrunk to that one brilliant idea—although his brain did not forget either how to run or how to shout in Greek, "Eureka!"

It seems that when we observe the world, we observe from a point of view located in some level in our hierarchies of control systems (to return to PCT). The world we experience is the world perceived by that level of the brain, or even only some part of that level. At one moment we can be admiring the shape of a sculpture, and at the next be aghast as its price. We can be focussed down on a full bladder, being unaware at that moment that the President is offering his hand. We can find ourselves turning the car into our home driveway, with no recollection of anything but a business problem that has been occupying us since we walked out the door at work—and we worry about how many red traffic lights we ignored on the way or how many collisions we barely avoided. And who has never found himself standing in front of a closet, wondering "Why am I standing here looking into this closet?"

I'm not about to tackle here the almost uninvestigated problems of how consciousness relates to brain operation. All we need here is one phenomenon of consciousness, the apparent fact that when we are being aware of something in the world of experience, we are not aware of the position from which we're consciously observing it. If we are looking for relationships, the world simply presents us with endless relationships like in, on, beside, above, parallel to, bigger than, and so forth. It doesn't occur to us that we are looking for relationships; they're just there. If we're aware of a conflict, we can see that doing one thing is conflicting with doing another, but it doesn't occur to us that we *want* both things to be occurring. We're aware of the problem, but at the moment, not of why it exists.

However, as many people have noticed, we are not entirely unaware of higher-level considerations. While we are focusing on some problem, so much that it seems to occupy all our attention, we can nevertheless have thoughts *about* what is going on, like "Gee, this is a tough problem." There is the level of experience in the foreground, the level that catches attention and seems the most important, and then there is a background of thoughts, attitudes, feelings, *about* the experience in the foreground. These background thoughts, as I will call them for short, are not central to what's going on; they're more like a running commentary on what is happening, a murmuring from another room.

The key to going up a level seems to be to shift attention to these background thoughts, the thoughts that are about the foreground activities, whether the foreground consists of other thoughts or simply things going on, like pulling on rubber bands. If you're busy trying to keep a knot on a dot, and also trying to keep the tension in the rubber bands from reaching a dangerous level, you might well be thinking, "This is really hard to do," or something like that. If, at that moment, you happened to notice that thought, and move it, as it were, to the center of attention for a moment, you might notice a lot of other thoughts going on, such as "This is really impossible—in fact, this can't be done. I'm not stupid, it's the task that's stupid. Do I have to keep doing this?" And before you know it, the answer to the last question comes up loud and clear: NO. So you stop doing it.

That's really all it takes to resolve a conflict. Remember our somewhat less than immortal fact: Reorganization follows awareness. When you move into the position from which you can see the level that is *setting* the goals, that level becomes subject to reorganization. With normal luck, it will take only a few reorganizations to alter the situation enough to eliminate the conflict. That's the theory, anyway. However, it also seems to work in practice. If you look at the practices of almost any psychotherapy, taking the term broadly, you will find there is almost no other problem to be solved but that of inner conflict, and that embedded in every technique somewhere, there is a way of getting people to go up a level, and see the problem from a new and higher point of view. Everything else, I might venture, is window-dressing and of little importance.

If I am to go by past experience, this is the point where someone will remind me of something other than these aspects of psychotherapy that is obviously of critical importance, but until that happens I will rest my case.

Chapter 7

Conflict
Between People

*In which we see that the main cause
of conflicts between people is the
attempt by one person
to control another*

Conflict Between People

Internal conflicts, although they can have serious consequences for the individual, can be relatively easy to resolve, given some help and a framework of theory in which to understand what is going on. The conflicting control systems are inside the same person; whichever way the solution goes, the same individual will benefit. When conflicts arise between two people, however, the best of all possible resolutions would leave both people better off, but that isn't as easy to achieve.

Let's begin working our way through this problem by stating what it is. A conflict between two people exists when the action used by one person to achieve or maintain a reference condition in perception causes a perception in another person to deviate significantly from the reference condition in the other person. In other words, the actions I use to get what I want prevent you from getting what you want. It's a true conflict if this works both ways—if your getting what you want likewise prevents me from getting what I want. The two people trying to pull the knot so it is over two different dots is the essence of the situation.

As we saw at the beginning of the previous chapter, conflict between people can lead automatically to conflict inside one or both people. The person who is most afraid of breaking the rubber bands goes into conflict first and can no longer keep pulling harder, so the other, bolder, person wins—the knot goes over the other person's dot. This is a very common outcome of conflicts between people, from a poker player jumping the bet to drive the other players out of the hand to nations at war escalating the intensity of fighting or using ever-more-horrible weapons to destroy the other side's "will to resist." The player or the side who first sees that trying harder will cause more error than it corrects will go into internal conflict, and become unable to try still harder. The poker player who is sure he has a winning hand finds that his pile of chips is shrinking more than he is willing to permit, so he finds himself unwilling to match or raise the next big bet, and folds. The nation that is sure it can win the war with just a little more effort goes into conflict between losing still more of its people and resources and launching yet another large offensive—and is quickly driven to defeat by the nation willing and able to risk more.

Every successful poker player, military strategist, politician, businessman, or criminal understands this aspect of conflict between people. As many of them will explain, what wins conflicts is not just having the greater resources (although that certainly helps); what is absolutely required is the willingness to keep raising the ante regardless of the risk—being willing to risk more than the other guy before internal conflict, otherwise known as prudence, puts a limit on the effort.

But this chapter is not about how to win conflicts. It's about understanding conflicts between people and resolving them. There is a lot I would like to say about conflict as the basis of a social system—about the enormous disadvantages of a system designed so that a large part of the efforts of some people are used only to cancel the effects of the efforts of other people. These disadvantages are just as great when the conflict is between people as when they are inside an individual, and for essentially the same reasons.

But to go into that subject would risk turning this into a political discussion in an area where discussion quickly becomes a flaming argument. Even more to the point, it would involve airing things I have opinions about because I am human and have to live in a society, but which I am just as ignorant about as the next person. I am only a theoretician here, working out the implications of a theory of human nature—not a sociologist or political scientist or economic guru. It would be easy to give the impression that because I say one way of life suffers from the crippling effects of conflict, I am recommending some other way of life—if I criticize capitalism, I must be in favor of socialism, for example. But there is no social system I know of (that is big enough for me to know about it) that doesn't suffer to a great or a greater degree the effects of conflict among people. So the main thing here is to understand conflict itself.

Conflict arises first because we are all autonomous control systems—it is our nature to seek goals and oppose disturbances; and second because there is so little understanding of our nature as control systems. The most important thing is to understand conflict; how it arises out of our nature as control systems, what its effects are, and how it can be resolved. If it happens that you want to win conflicts rather than resolve them, understanding the nature of conflict might lead you to win more easily, or even change your mind in some instances. If you want to resolve conflicts, the same understanding will help with that, too. I can try to convey understanding, but I can't make up your mind for you.

Why We Have Conflicts

People are control systems, which is to say that they develop goals and take action to make the perceived world match the goals. They have not one goal, but many, and the goals exist not at just one level but many. The basic problem of social living is the one outlined at the start of this chapter: The actions people generate, even innocently, to achieve their own goals often disturb other people's control processes. Even just trying to get into a vacant theater seat so you can watch a movie entails your blocking someone else's view, if only for a few seconds. We bump into each other, step on each other's toes, and in general interfere with each other at every turn.

But, fortunately, people *are* control systems, which means that ordinary disturbances that tend to interfere with control are quickly handled by adjustments of our own actions. When someone steps into a rowboat, rocking it, the other people in the boat don't go pitching over the side; they just lean a little and keep their balance. People are *good* control systems; they handle the effects of disturbances, for the most part, automatically, not even needing to think about them. Watch a crowd of city dwellers moving along the sidewalks as the working day is about to start. They don't bounce off one person after another or come to violent stops in face-to-face collisions. They snake their way between approaching people, mutually avoiding collisions, and the opposing mobs magically filter their way through each other with scarcely a brushed sleeve. They all get where they want to go, without keeping anyone else from doing the same.

When you begin to notice all the little disturbances that come and go in ordinary behavior, ordinary interactions with other people, you begin to see that our ability to control is continuously at work, and that practically all of the time it keeps collisions and confrontations and frustrations from ever happening. We just do a little sidestep, correct our balance, and keep going. No big deal.

It's only our nature as control systems that lets us live together at all. When we eat together, we have conventions such as "your fork" and "my fork" that do away with our reaching for the same fork at the same time and ending up wrestling on the floor for possession. We each control something that the other person isn't also trying to control, and so we easily and naturally avoid the scenes that are common among three-year-olds. It's really only in the rarest instances that we come into true conflict, grabbing for the last fork and trying to wrest it away from the other person. Our own higher-level systems, which are concerned with such things as smooth social interaction and self-image, quickly resolve the problem by changing the immediate goals at the lower levels. The President and the Prime Minister are certainly not going to get into a wrestling match over the last fork at the buffet table. If anything, they will have a comical little conflict over who gets to let the other person have it. After all, they know that someone will quickly hand them a fork if they don't end up with one.

The normal human condition in social situations, as in all others, is to avoid direct conflict. This is usually possible because the environment, a real environment outside the behavioral laboratory, is rich in alternative ways to achieve the same end. If there's construction going on at the entrance to a side street, you don't find people lined up for miles in their cars waiting for the construction to be finished. They find a different route and get where they're going anyway. If you can't find the doorstop, you use a book or a shoe or a laptop computer. If someone's using the phone booth, you go to the next phone booth, or decide to send a fax, or decide it can wait until you get home. If there were one and only one action that would achieve each goal we have, we would be in big trouble.

It's uncommon for a conflict to persist for very long. There are just too many ways in which we can change what doesn't matter to us, or matters less, in order to keep control of what does matter, or matters more. Conflicts, true inescapable conflicts, are therefore rare. Or rather, they are rare when they result merely from a combination of circumstances that happens to remove all of the alternative ways to sidestep it. When it is only bad luck that creates the conflict, both parties to it have every reason to focus attention on it and work out a way to resolve it with no fuss.

When conflict with another person threatens to occur, the first automatic reaction is to look for a simple way around it. We all understand that conflict is inconvenient, distracting, and expensive. When you're walking along the sidewalk, and another person walks toward you, you change your path a little to show which way you're going to go to avoid the collision, hardly paying any attention. If the other person moves the same way, you might take evasive action again, which the other person might do at the same time, leading to a little chuckle as you recognize the familiar impasse that comes from the inability to read minds. It may take you quite a while to realize that the other person is deliberately standing in front of you with a peculiar smile on her face and keeping you from going on, and to recognize that thing in her hand as a gun.

It's not normal for one person to deliberately create a conflict with another person, in the sense that this isn't what we normally expect to happen outside the context of a game. And even people who, in effect, deliberately create a conflict may not realize that this is what they're doing. Even the woman with the gun doesn't expect you to be (like Jack Benny) in conflict when she offers you the choice, "Your money or your life." Jack, a world-class skinflint, said, "I'm thinking, I'm thinking," but you would probably just hand over the money.

That's a quickly-resolved conflict, but its cause is not, in general, so easily removed. Behind this kind of conflict there is the prime source of conflict between people: one person trying to control another.

People Controlling People

People are control systems, acting on their worlds only to make their perceptions match the reference perceptions that they have chosen. And people are *hierarchies* of control systems, in which reference perceptions at one level are adjusted so as to make more general, higher-level, perceptions match higher-level goal states. Moreover, they are "massively parallel" control systems, in which many perceptions at each level are adjusted to make many higher-level perceptions match many reference conditions at the same time. One nice thing about PCT is that it shows how such a complex system can be built up, level by level, so that actions on the world can actually manage to bring all these perceptions at all these levels to the states that are desired at a given moment. It's not nearly as improbable as it sounds.

These human control systems act on the environment to make it conform to what they want to perceive at many levels. They become very good at this by the time they are adults. But a basic problem arises when the things they are trying to control are not pencils and telephones and cars and plants, but other people.

We can't literally control "other people." That covers too much territory. And anyway, all we really want to control is their behavior—what they do that impacts on us. When someone is standing on our collective foot, we don't want to control that person's religion, we just want the person to stand somewhere else. So we give the person a mighty shove, and that makes the pain in our foot go away.

We could, of course, use less violent means; we might say "Please get off our foot." We might even rely on the person's own social perceptions and empathy, and simply say "You're standing on our foot," leaving it to the other person to know what to do about that. In other words, we could treat the incident as an accident and assume that there is a will to resolve the conflict between different ideas of where this person should stand.

It's pretty hard to treat an incident as an accident, however, when you're a young woman being told by her boss, "Take your clothes off or lose your job," or a small businessman being told "We're going on strike unless you double our pay." Unfortunately, there are many people who do not realize that getting what they want may involve trying to cause another person to behave in a way that destroys that person's ability to stay in control of his or her own life. There are even people who positively relish the idea of being able to control someone else's behavior. There are people who think it is necessary to control other people's behavior, or that it is the sensible thing to do, or that they have a God-given right to do so. There are people who think that the best way to get something done is to give orders, to threaten, to micromanage, to bully or wheedle or withhold necessities or inflict bodily harm. What all this comes down to is that there are many people, many many people, who think that controlling other people's behavior is both possible and necessary, or even fun.

Sometimes they are right. If someone is coming at you with a knife, you very much need to control that person's behavior, and nobody is going to fault you for trying to do that. But usually they are wrong. They are wrong because if you succeed in controlling another person's behavior, or even come close, the most likely result is to create a continuing conflict.

This is not just because people don't like to be controlled. Sometimes they do like it. It's because no controller of another person can guess what they're doing to the whole intricate hierarchy of control systems when they try to make the other person produce a specific behavior that has nothing to do with what is needed to maintain control at all levels in that person's hierarchy—or even disrupts that control. Even if the other person is eager to follow orders, and sticks a finger in a light socket as commanded, the control systems in that person's brain are going to yank it right out again. In order to produce the commanded behavior, the person must enter into a serious internal conflict, and in most cases that will simply result in not following orders.

I will put this baldly: The primary cause of conflict between people is the attempt by some people to control the behavior of other people. It doesn't matter whether the means are nice or nasty: Nobody knows so much about the internal organization of another person that it is possible to dictate a behavior, or lack of behavior, that will not disturb something the other is controlling, and thus call forth opposition.

It is, of course, possible to negotiate with another person, and find out whether producing the behavior you want will cause that person any serious problems. If it will, the other person can ask what you want this change for, and perhaps come up with a different behavior that will accomplish the same thing as far as you are concerned.

But, when you negotiate, remember that people have not just one goal but a whole structure of goals, hierarchically arranged. When you demand a particular behavior before the person can get some wanted thing, the person may be willing, but performing that behavior may interfere with controlling something else of equal or greater importance to the person. If you want to control that person without resistance, you have to understand what all the other goals are and how they relate to each other. And seeking that understanding radically changes the relationship between you and the other.

When you try to control a person's behavior, that probably means that you want the person to stop doing something or start doing something else, something important to you. But if you understand even some of the other person's main goals and how they relate to that person's behavior, that implies a relationship with the other person completely different from the relationship between controller and controllee. You will understand why the person is doing what you don't want, or not doing what you do want. You will see, moreover, that the other person's behavior is completely reasonable and necessary from that person's point of view, just as reasonable and necessary as your own behavior seems to you. Now it is impossible to remain a reasonable person and simply demand that the other behave as you wish. The only reasonable course left is to negotiate. Negotiation is the main alternative to controlling others.

Negotiation implies the possibility that either party or both will reorganize and change reference conditions. Now rather than unilaterally deciding what the other is to do, and withholding rewards until you get what you want, you have to try to strike a bargain. You make a proposal: If you will change what you want in some specific way to give me at least some of what I want, I will change at least some of what I want to give you at least some of what you want. Now the situation has become symmetrical; the playing field is level. Two equal parties are trying to strike a deal that will make the experiences of each one more like the experiences they want to have. If the right clever deal is conceived of during this interaction, both parties can be better off than before. This is what is known to the touchie-feelie lump-in-the-throat crowd as a "win-win situation." It is known to PCTers as the only practical basis for a sustainable social system.

So there is no insuperable obstacle to getting other people to behave in ways you want or need. The world is rich in alternative ways to get to any particular end; all you have to do is explore them and persuade others that there is something to be gained from helping you.

Rubber bands: As long as you're willing, as the experimenter, to let the other person keep the knot over the dot, you can put that person's end of the rubber bands anywhere you want it just by moving your end around—as long as you don't run the other person's hand into a hot object, or otherwise inconvenience the other person. Try it.

However, in order to handle the situation this way, one has to give up the idea of simply *controlling the other person*. And that can be very hard to do, especially if you don't really understand how people work. It seems risky to leave the other person in charge of his or her own behavior, when that behavior is important to you.

There is, on the other hand, no real alternative, unless you're ready to back up your control of the other person with threats or force. And that leads to the kind of conflict that escalates, that festers, that produces more frustration and cost than you are likely to want to bear. Of course if you just think "that's life," you will bear the cost and the frustration and muddle through, but the result won't be anything like what it could be without the conflict.

People controlling people: That's the problem. And it's mainly caused by ignorance, not, usually, ill-will. It's caused by not understanding the difference between an inanimate object and a living system. Inanimate objects don't push back when you push on them; they either just sit there, if they're too heavy to move, or they move. If you push on a big rock and it doesn't move, you push harder. You keep pushing harder until either you give up because it's not worth the pain, or the rock moves. Once it's moved, it stays moved. So naturally, when you have a problem getting another person to move the way you want, you just push harder. It's a no-brainer. You don't recognize that there's a brain in there, doing essentially the same thing you're doing, as determined not to move as you are that it will move. Even if you prevail, this living object may well do something that a rock would never do: The first time you turn your back, it brings a club down on your head.

I imagine that cavemen might have been puzzled at the failure of other people to behave like rocks, but since they did manage to live together they must have had at least a glimmer of the difference. Ten or a hundred thousand years later, their descendants probably have more of a glimmer, but now, I think, they may be ready to make the final leap to understanding: that controlling other people basically doesn't work. It just creates conflict.

Me not rock—OK, Og? A bumper sticker for the new millennium.

Resolving Conflict Between People

There are, fortunately, many people who greatly prefer resolving conflicts over winning them, and many who spend their lives helping others to do the same. I hope they recognize in this chapter, and in PCT, some basic principles that they already know intuitively.

The resolution of conflicts between people is much like the resolution of conflict within an individual. There is the level where the conflict is expressed: where the actions of one person come into direct opposition to the actions of another person. There is the level where the conflict is caused: where two goals exist, such that for one person to achieve one goal is to prevent the other from reaching the other goal. And there is the level that creates the situation in which the goals are incompatible.

In the usual course of affairs, it is the lowest level that grabs our attention first: the battle itself, the protesters throwing bottles at the cops and the cops pushing back with missile shields, water cannons, and tear gas. It all looks mindless and senseless, until you step back a pace and consider what each side is trying to accomplish. The cops have the goal of restoring law and order, the protestors want to create enough of a ruckus, by technically illegal means, to call attention to their demands for liberty and justice.

If we take that one step back, we see that floating above the battle there are two sets of reference conditions that can't be satisfied at the same time. And when we step back again, we see that above even this level there is another: the situation that makes law and order seem incompatible with liberty and justice. It is only after the second step back that we begin to see where minds might be changed, where reorganization might accomplish something to change the situation. If our postulate about reorganization following awareness holds true, the objective in resolving the battle in the streets must be to direct attention to this third level up, the level where the application of human ingenuity and creativity can make a change that makes the conflict irrelevant. Not "win" it, or "settle" it, but change the situation in such a way that the goals are no longer in conflict. Is it really necessary to choose between law and order on the one hand, and freedom and justice on the other? Does anybody really want to preserve a situation that prevents these goals from coexisting?

If the answer to that last question is "yes," then we need to go up another level by asking why. It does no good to wrangle at one level when the problem is at a higher level. If you have your lawyer consult my lawyer, you will find that I postulated that there are *at least* three levels involved in a conflict. There may be more. The resolution of conflict, in or between people, requires moving attention to the level where change is possible.

In some unlicensed and informal experiments with friends and acquaintances, I have done some explorations of what happens when the level of attention is changed inside a single person. These experiments were not particularly aimed at resolving conflicts inside a person, but when you ask a person to describe what is in the background of anything the person wants to talk about, attention does seem to go up a level, and after a few repetitions of this one inevitably stumbles across conflicts. Pursuing the same principle of calling attention to background ideas, attitudes, thoughts, and so on has some remarkable effects when conflicts are encountered. Quite often, the first thing to change is the emotional content of the discussion; the upsetting thought that sprang up, sometimes to the tune of anger or despair, becomes the subject of the conversation, and suddenly the emotion is gone like turning off a switch. And if the process is continued, again quite often, the conflict simply disappears. The person says, in effect, "Well, right now that doesn't seem to be so much of a problem." And it isn't. An obvious solution has appeared.

This, of course, is what we hope to accomplish when conflicts between people arise. I expect that there are experts in the field of conflict resolution who do something like this as a matter of course; it's obvious that the conflicting parties have to view the situation from a position where they can see what needs to be changed. The main difference from doing this by questioning a single individual is that *two* people (or more) must start operating consciously at the higher level, and *both* must reorganize.

I apologize for making this sound easier than it is, but you must remember that we are making deductions from a theory, not discussing practical realities. If it should turn out that the theory suggests processes that have, in fact, been found to fit with practical procedures, this tends to give us more confidence in the theory, and perhaps to see in its simplified principles something that could be carried along into practical applications.

In fact, where these principles have been consciously tried in practical situations, they seem to produce interesting results. In the Reference section, Tom Bourbon reviews what has happened in a number of school systems where these PCT principles have been applied to the problem of classroom discipline, in a program conceived and taught by Edward Ford, a long-time supporter of PCT. Discipline problems are, of course, conflicts: The students and the teacher or administrator do not agree on how the student should behave. The mere fact that they are called "discipline" problems shows that the customary approach involves control of one person by another—which is what generates the conflicts. Ford's Responsible Thinking Program teaches the basic principles of PCT to everyone in the school system, in a framework of simple and consistent procedures that are easy to teach and learn. For example, the question, "What are you doing?" (if asked as a genuine request for a description) can jog a student (or a teacher!) up a level sufficiently to cut a potential incident short.

When parents, teachers, students, administrators, cafeteria workers, bus drivers, and security personnel all learn these principles and how to apply them, the result can be quite impressive—even in juvenile-offender lockup facilities. At the very least, the PCT approach to conflict between people seems to be worthy of further development. Have a look at Ford's work in the Reference.

Chapter 8

Reward
and Punishment

*In which we see that the idea of
reward and punishment
stems from a misunderstanding of
human nature and a desire
to control other people*

Reward and Punishment

You better watch out,

You better not cry,

You better not pout,

I'm telling you why,

Santa Claus is coming to town.

At one time, psychologists who wanted to control other people's behavior thought that objects and events like candy or praise had inherent rewarding properties. If you administered a reward while someone was acting the way you wanted, or closer to it, the reward would "strengthen" the tendency to repeat that behavior.

The reason that psychologists thought reward works this way was that everyone thought it works this way. Reward and punishment were not inventions of psychology: They were part of folk wisdom handed down through the ages. Reward and punishment have always been thought of as means by which one person can control the behavior of another—a subject about which you probably know more now than you did two chapters ago. People do want to control each other; sometimes they really need to control others, sometimes it is profitable to do so, sometimes it gives one a sense of power and competence, sometimes it seems to be the only way to keep an orderly society. If it weren't for the need or desire to control others, the ideas of reward and punishment would probably never have arisen.

It's easy to see why not. Just consider reward from the standpoint of the person being rewarded (punishment is another subject that we'll get into later). If someone said, "I'll give you this five-dollar bill to tie my shoes for me," and if you didn't get instantly suspicious that this is the beginning of some kind of trick (perhaps the shoes in question are in Nome, Alaska), you'd probably do it. Why not? It's an easy five bucks for a trivial amount of work. [All right: Residents of Nome, Alaska, please read: Rio de Janeiro].

But we have to ask what made you tie the shoes. Was it something in the five-dollar bill that acted on your nervous system to cause you to kneel down and manipulate those little strings just so? Did the image of that five-dollar bill on your retinas cause a lot of neural signals to spread through your brain and finally reach your muscles and cause those tying movements? That's pretty much what a lot of psychological and common sense uses of the term reward seem to be asking us to believe.

But suppose that the same person said, "Now I'll give you another five-dollar bill to *untie* my shoes." You'd probably do that, too. Now we have a five-dollar bill causing exactly the opposite behavior. The same object can cause you to do one thing, or the opposite. What kind of "cause" is that? Thinking this way can raise some interesting questions, and make us wonder whether a reward actually causes us to do anything at all.

From the standpoint of the person being rewarded, this whole discussion is leaving out something vital. What it is would be evident immediately if our poor fat person who can't bend over far enough to tie his own shoes were to say, "I'll give you this wrinkled rectangle of dirty white paper to tie my shoes." In that case, if we comply it will be only because we feel sorry for the person. Who wants a wrinkled rectangle of dirty white paper?

What does "want" mean? It means two things: that there is a reference condition specifying an amount of something, and that one wants—lacks—it (or has something like pain that one wants not to have, but let's stick to one simple case). In the case of the five-dollar bill, you may want money, but have less of it than you want, so you "want" it in both senses—you desire it and you lack it. When a means is presented for making the difference between what you want and what you have—the error signal, remember?—a little smaller, you will use this means (if it's not painful or too costly in other ways). The act specified for getting the reward is a means of controlling something that matters to you—something you both desire and do not have enough of.

So if you want the five-dollar bill you will do what is needed to get it. The fat man wants his shoes tied (or untied) and giving the five-dollar bill is his somewhat extravagant way of satisfying that reference condition. Evidently the fat man has so much money that losing five dollars causes less sense of error than does having his shoelaces in the wrong state.

This is a perfectly simple PCT description of the transaction. The fat man uses giving the five dollars as his means of getting his shoes tied, and you use tying his shoes as your means of getting the five dollars. A perfect fit, two control systems interacting in a way that corrects both of their error signals!

But what has happened to the idea of "reward"? What is the fat man *doing* to you to *make* you tie his shoes? That notion has quietly flitted out the window. That's not at all what is happening. If people had understood this sort of transaction as a simple interaction between two control systems, enabling both of them to get what they want by performing some action, the concept of "giving rewards" would never have been invented. Of course control theory wasn't a subject even in engineering schools until the late 1930s, so a lot of development of human culture went on before that without an understanding of control to help explain things.

But hold on, there's more to the story than that. There is a hierarchy of control. If you could get inside the fat man, perhaps you would find (at a higher level) that he gets a big kick out of handing someone five bucks to tie his shoes. If you do tie his shoes, he may then offer you ten bucks to kiss them. It doesn't take many examples of this sort to get the idea across that the fat man thinks he has control of you. Wave some money around, and you can get people to do anything you want. "Watch this: Hey, boy, wanna make an easy five bucks?"

Obviously the relationship would not be very satisfying to this particular fat man if the shoe-tier had approached him saying "Tie your shoes for five bucks, mister?" The fat man wouldn't give five cents for that and he'd probably be insulted on top of it; the point is who is going to control whom, not whether shoes get tied or money changes hands. A reward is what you use to *make* people do things. The moment you think of the reward as something another person *made* you give, the thrill is gone, or it has changed sides. This is why some businessmen hate unions with a blindly furious passion. The union workers are trying to make the businessmen *give* the same rewards that the businessmen want to *use* for controlling the workers. It's not the money or the working conditions that's at stake: It's who is in control here.

So the idea of reward is largely a product of a society in which people think they have to control other people to get what they want. Practically every society that has ever existed has thought this, those that haven't simply used overwhelming physical force without thinking about it, to make others do their bidding, as people did in slave societies like ancient Greece. This doesn't have to imply a psychological struggle between egos as in the example of our fat man; if people think this is how human nature works, they will simply act accordingly. And, before control theory, this is how most people have understood human nature. It's a matter of how you interpret experience.

Science and Reward

If you believe that you have to control other people to survive, then it's only human to believe that you *can* control other people. This means that you are likely to believe in the efficacy of reward, especially since it's easy to interpret experience in a way that seems to support this belief.

If everybody has believed in the efficacy of reward for many generations, it should not be surprising that scientists who grew up with the same belief should discover that not only can people administer rewards as a way of controlling behavior, but the inanimate environment can do the same thing. The scientists, not wanting to use a simple lay term, called rewards *reinforcers*, things which increase the probability that the behavior that caused them will occur again. This shifts attention from the person using the reward for controlling others to the rewarding object itself, as if the rewardingness resided in the object. And they saw that reinforcers could be given not just by one person to another person, but by nonliving objects and events in the environment. If going through doors is reinforcing, then the act of twisting the knob and pulling on it leads to the opening of the door and going through it, which reinforces the acts of twisting and pulling. The door is now in control of your behavior.

How does a scientist prove that going through doors is reinforcing? Basically, there is no proof; only a description of what happens. If a toddler at first can't open doors, the scientist may help by turning the knob and pulling a little so the toddler can complete the job and stagger through the door. Once this has happened a few times, the toddler begins trying to turn the knob and pull because—as the scientist would say—that response to the sight of a closed door has become strengthened by success in going through the door. A little success rewards or reinforces the tendency to twist and pull the next time the closed door is encountered, until finally the toddler opens the door every time. (The scientist's wife, of course, cries "You taught her to do *what?*" as little Mary toddles purposefully toward the door to the basement staircase.)

This isn't a proof; it's just an interpretation, a way of talking about what happens as the child learns to open the door. To support this idea the scientist has to imagine some rewarding effect of going through the door that somehow reaches inside the child and cranks up the tendency to twist the knob and pull on it. The idea that the child *wants* to go through the door, and tries different kinds of behavior until it can do so, didn't seem to impress the scientists who thought up the idea of reinforcement. It made more sense somehow, to have the environment controlling people than to have people controlling themselves and the environment. In a world where practically everyone thought that controlling people is necessary and good, such a theory looked perfectly reasonable. With millions of people controlling millions of other people every day, how much credibility would a psychologist have had if he or she announced that people don't actually control other people, and maybe shouldn't try?

This view of behavior and reward is no longer dominant in psychology, although those who support it may think it is. However, it still dominates popular concepts of behavior in business, education, law, and child-rearing, not to mention common sense. To displace it we need a large number of people who understand PCT and can explain what is wrong with reward as the basis for interactions among people.

Preconditions for Reward

PCT gives us an understanding of "reward" that can also show us some of the drawbacks of this concept of human interaction. X is rewarding to a person only if the person desires X, and does not have X, or as much of X as is wanted. This implies certain preliminaries if you happen to have control of X and want to use it as a reward in controlling someone else's behavior. Let's make a list.

First, of course, you have to be pretty sure that the person wants some X. He has to have a current reference condition set for some nonzero amount of X.

Second, you have to make sure that the person does not already have enough X to satisfy the reference condition.

Third, you must be sure that what you're asking the other person to do in order to get some X doesn't violate some other reference condition in the other person—cause pain or embarrassment or excessive fatigue, or interfere with controlling something else in the person's life, the action thus producing more error than it corrects. Or, if you don't care about this problem, you have to have enough physical force at your disposal to overcome any objections of this sort.

Fourth, you have to be sure that the person can't get some X by doing something else that is quicker and easier—for example, just by asking someone else for some X without having to do anything in return.

And fifth, you have to be sure there are some safeguards in place so the other person can't just take the X away from you as soon as he finds out you have it or can give it.

If you test these preconditions against any situation in which someone gives you rewards to get you to do something—for example, a case where someone gives you a paycheck (X = $) for doing certain work—you will see that all these conditions are satisfied.

Consider rewarding a rat in a cage for pressing a bar by giving it food (X = food pellets). Condition 1 is met by physiology:

Rats have a built-in reference condition for food intake. Condition 2 is established by withholding food for some time, long enough to be sure the rat does not have as much food intake as it wants. The third condition is established by the schedule of reinforcement and the spring tension under the lever: If the action required to get the food is too complicated or the bar is too hard to press, the rat will give up and starve to death. The fourth condition is established by keeping the rat in an escape-proof cage, with no other source of food available. And the fifth condition is the most easily met: The experimenter is so big and strong in comparison with the rat that the rat has no way of wresting the food out of the experimenter's hands; the apparatus is so strong that the rat can't tear it apart to get at the food.

Built-In Problems with Reward as a Means of Control

The point of mentioning these preconditions is that all but the first require the giver of rewards to have a considerable degree of control over the rewardee before the process ever starts. This is as evident in the case of a human being as it is in that of a rat.

Human beings do have needs and wants. Normally they act in ways that would keep those reference conditions satisfied. However, if people were really able to maintain their worlds close to the reference conditions they want, they would be almost unrewardable. What do you give the man who has everything he wants? Would a millionaire tie your shoes for five bucks, or kiss them for ten? Obviously, people are the most rewardable, and the most controllable through rewards, when they have difficulty getting what they want or need and even have chronic unsatisfied needs.

A person who is convinced that it is necessary to control others on a wide scale, therefore, finds that it is to his or her advantage to make sure that there are many people with unsatisfied needs or wants. Since people are control systems, they will try very hard to satisfy their needs—the greater the need, up to a point, the harder they will try. The limit comes when the very effort to correct the error costs more than success could possibly benefit the person. A person or an animal will run around looking for food over a wide territory, but when the energy burned in the search becomes greater than the available food can supply, the running around has to cease. The animal or person gives up, conserving energy, perhaps in the hope that something will change before starvation ends it all. So the person who wants to control by using rewards would not want everyone to be in such an extreme state of deprivation that the cost of the effort needed to get the reward would exceed the benefits. The ideal state for controllability is for people to be working as hard as they can just to maintain the status quo. If they had to work any harder they would begin to give up; if they worked any less hard, you could still get more work out of them.

This condition is tricky to maintain because when there is deprivation, people will be looking everywhere for a means to reduce it. If you have control of the food supply, you can withhold food until people are pretty willing to work to get some, but if you withhold too much, or make it too hard to get food, the people will start trying to grow it themselves or steal it. This will happen long before the critical point is reached, or what is called maximum productivity. So it's necessary to take steps to prevent people from finding other means of satisfying their needs without doing what you want from them. If you have the clout, you can pass laws that forbid the growing of food without a certificate of purity, and then make such certificates almost impossible for anyone else to obtain. You can easily get laws against stealing passed. And once you have a law, you can call on superior physical force to keep people from breaking it. This leaves only one option: to do what you want.

What we're talking about here, of course, is just the usual way in which civilized societies are organized. Even without Machiavellian calculation going on, this is the natural result of trying to control other people, and trying to do it by means of rewards. To establish and maintain the conditions under which people can be controlled by rewards, it's necessary to set up a despotism in which the rich and powerful, or simply the unscrupulous, have the means to satisfy people's needs, and the power to prevent those people from finding other ways to satisfy their needs. A system of government, law, or brute force is required in the background, so that people who try to satisfy their needs without doing what is demanded of them are curbed by physical force.

When we look coolly at the reward-based society, the picture that results is enough to make a flaming Libertarian out of anybody, or a Socialist or a Communist or any sort of revolutionary. It's clearly a rotten system and needs to be torn down and replaced—by something or other. The only problem is that every time a revolution occurs and the despots are thrown out, when a new system is built up and everything is running again it works just like the old one. People still believe they need to control other people, they still find rewards the only practical way to control them, and they still end up developing a means of keeping people from satisfying their needs through unofficial channels—which boils down to having laws and a police force to enforce them. "Revolution" is an apt term for the process of throwing the bastards out: Everyone mills around in a big circle and ends up right where they started, socially speaking. The flag may have changed and the names of the political parties (or party) may have changed, but the new system is still based on people controlling people, backed up by physical force.

Maybe the lesson we should learn from this is that no matter what you call the system, people are still going to be trying to control each other, and we should just accept that and try to do it well. But maybe it's worth trying to see if there isn't some up-a-level solution that doesn't just send us around in those messy circles back to where we started.

The PCT Solution

What would happen, one wonders, if we simply abolished the idea of reward, and substituted the PCT interpretation of human interactions? You'll remember how simple it was: The fat man gave a five-dollar bill as his means of getting his shoe tied, and the shoe-tier tied the shoe as his means of getting five dollars. This doesn't change what actually happened; it doesn't even change the particular fat man's feeling of power over the other person. But it's a foot in the door.

When you look at it this way, it's easy to see that neither person *made* the other person do anything. If the fat man's offer were turned down, he could just look elsewhere for someone willing to make the deal. If the shoe-tier didn't want to tie the shoes, he could find a different way to get five bucks, from someone else or even by offering a different good or service to the fat man. "Hey, man, wanna buy a Rolex for $5?" Maybe the fat man is dumb, too.

The question is, do we really want to give up the idea of forcing other people to behave as we want them to behave? That's what the PCT solution boils down to. If you understand PCT, this isn't anything revolutionary; it's just a simple truth: People control their own experiences. The only way you can truly force them to behave as you wish is through the threat or actuality of overwhelmingly superior physical force—and even that's only a temporary solution unless you throw them in a cage or kill them. If that's the sort of society you want, good luck—but you'd better watch your back.

So what is this "PCT solution"? It's just a change in the way we understand human nature. We don't throw anything or anybody out; we don't try to change human behavior by force. We don't change the political system, or the economic system; those are consequences of the way people think of human nature, not causes. There are lots of political and economic systems that would probably work perfectly well, if people only understood how people really work.

If you've organized your life around an idea that seems to make a lot of sense, and then discover that it's actually causing most of the problems you want to solve, you're bound to feel a little foolish. People don't like to feel foolish: It undermines their self-confidence. We have to feel confident that we can handle whatever life throws at us; otherwise we'd just hole up in a cave and wait for it to be over. So what will happen as people realize that they've been working with a wrong concept of human nature? If they really understand that it's wrong, and see a concept that makes more sense out of more experiences, they won't want to go on in the old way. Everything that developed out of the old way depends on continuing to think in the old way, so if they change their minds, everything they do will change.

It won't change in one Big Bang, in a violent revolution once more around the circle; one little thing after another will change. If you know that people really can't be controlled by any means you would like to see in general use, this means that *you* can't be controlled except by extreme means. And it means that you don't *want* people to be controlled, not only because it's basically impossible in any reasonable world, but because you don't want to contribute toward a system in which *you* could be controlled.

This new point of view will cause all kinds of problems because you will keep running into the same situations that have always been handled before by trying to control people, and the solution will take time to work out. You'll still yell at your kids even while you're telling yourself "This isn't going to work out." If you like football you'll still get a thrill of vicarious power when your team crushes the opposition.

But in the back of your mind, you'll have a little virus working called PCT. It will whisper to your inner ear, "You didn't *make* him do that; he's trying to get what he wants and that's why he did it." This will start to undermine your rationalizations; they will gradually crumble away at the base. You'll start to get a new appreciation of what it can mean to say that all people are created equal. They all work the same way. They're all doing their best to make the worlds they experience be what they want to experience. They're just like you.

I've changed my mind. I'm not even going to talk about punishment. If you understand PCT, you can work out for yourself what's wrong with it. It's just reward stood on its head, and it's based on the same desire to control other people.

Chapter 9

Where Do We Go From Here?

*In which we see PCT
as a new direction for the
development of psychology*

Where Do We Go from Here?

Engineers invented control theory while trying to build machines that could imitate human beings controlling things. The basic concept and the principles of control theory have been around since the 1930s, when electronics was just starting to develop devices that did something beside play music or send messages. It's unfortunate that control systems weren't invented six decades earlier, or that psychology didn't wait another 60 years to turn into a laboratory science. A lot of trouble might have been avoided, and control theory might have started moving toward center stage in the life sciences a lot sooner.

What did happen was that the life sciences, lacking the central explanatory principle that is absolutely essential for understanding how organisms work, went ahead and tried to explain behavior anyway. The only model available during the last part of the 19th Century and the first part of the 20th was Newtonian physics, in which natural processes go from cause to effect in a simple straight line. Biologists, and after them psychologists, thought that the behavior of organisms could be explained in the same causal terms. Behavior, they thought, was the result of external influences acting on organisms, largely through their sensory nerves, just as masses are caused to move by external forces. It was thought that explaining behavior was just a matter of observing environmental conditions and seeing how they caused or altered the actions of organisms. If you had a big catalogue of stimulus conditions and the behaviors known to follow them, you could predict how any organism would behave, and by manipulating the environment, control that behavior. Psychologists were fascinated by the idea of predicting and controlling behavior—possibly more fascinated by the idea of controlling it since they had only slight success with predicting it.

We've seen now that perception, intention, comparison, error, and action are the essential ingredients of control, and that the basic principle of control is control of perception, not action. This makes the early development of psychology all the more ironic, for while psychologists spoke freely of controlling the behavior of their subjects, they did not see in those subjects any capacity to control anything. They failed to see that when scientists selected some behavior of an animal or person as a state to be brought about, and acted as necessary to achieve that state, they, the scientists, were working according to principles completely different from the principles they used to explain the behavior of their subjects. The result was a massive and apparently unconscious application of the rule, "Don't do as I do, do as I say."

The development of psychology took place much too soon, with the result that by the time the principles of control theory were developed, psychology had gone far down a different road, trying as hard as possible to explain behavior in terms of environmental causes. In fact, by the 1930s the central core of scientific psychology had considered and rejected as an illusion the possibility that organisms could select goals and intentionally pursue them. Even the word "intention" had been stolen away from its previous common (and correct) usage, and given a new philosophically obscure meaning. The conclusion that purpose does not exist had become set in concrete, with the result that when control theory came along and showed us exactly how purposive or goal-directed behavior could work in a real physical brain, the implicit message was not only overlooked, but was actively resisted and rejected by the mainstream with scornful cries of "mysticism!"

Almost immediately after control theory was invented, engineers began building control systems to do all sorts of things, and at the same time a few non-engineers noticed that these new "servomechanisms" and "regulators" behaved in ways that made them look alive (not realizing that this was the original intention). The engineers, had they been interested in such things, might have been gratified at this acknowledgment of their success at reproducing the behavior of the living systems they were trying to imitate. But when Arturo Rosenbleuth pointed out the similarity of certain servomechanisms to known mechanisms in the human body, and when Norbert Wiener expanded this insight into a new discipline he called "cybernetics," the impact on psychology was essentially zero. It was even negative; psychologists objected loudly that human beings are not machines.

And they are not machines—not the kinds of machines which were the only ones that psychologists understood. The barriers to acceptance of control theory went higher because not only were psychologists being told that they had overlooked a fundamental principle of behavioral organization, but that this essential principle, when it was finally unearthed, hadn't even been discovered by a psychologist. Well actually it had been discovered by a psychologist in the 1890s, William James, but there was no formal analysis available then and nothing came of it.

That was the situation at mid-century when cybernetics started its brief decade in the sun (and when I began my interest in control theory). By the early 1960s, it was clear that psychology had successfully fended off this threat; cybernetics had turned into philosophy, and Skinnerian behaviorism was in the saddle, at least in America where I have always lived. The computer revolution had begun and the human brain was thought to operate like a big stimulus-response machine. Those who were interested in control theory were always around, but always on the periphery, scratching for support and a scientific audience.

I had worked on understanding control theory for twenty years, had developed a fairly complete theory, and had published a book on the subject before I began to understand just why control theory had been so slow to be accepted. It had never occurred to me that if control theory was the right approach, then essentially *everything* that psychology had apparently discovered about human behavior was probably wrong. Not totally everything, of course, but so nearly everything that the only way for control theory to be accepted was for psychology to start over, essentially from scratch. I then realized that this conclusion had probably been evident to many psychologists long before it dawned on me.

As you have been reading through this book, you may have noticed the virtual absence of certain terms such as habits, tendencies, stimuli, responses, conditioning, trauma, personality, and instincts—all those words that have grown up inside and around psychology. Imagine, then, how this theory that is now called PCT must have sounded to professional psychologists. Here was a theory that purported to explain behavior in great detail, considering all aspects of it from spinal reflexes to activities we would now call cognitive, without ever mentioning most of the categories which conventional psychologists need even to talk about behavior, not to mention understand it. Control theory deals with most of the same phenomena with which psychologists have been concerned—but from a totally different set of premises. The mere existence of this theory had to be an affront to a century of psychological "progress."

Another twenty years have now gone by since I finally understood the problem. In that time, a slowly expanding core of scientists and other professionals has grown up in support of control theory—one of them, the sociologist Kent McClelland, was responsible for labeling our new approach "Perceptual Control Theory" or PCT. One of the main results has been a shift of attitudes. For over two decades I tried to express the theory in neutral terms, not attacking mainstream psychology but thinking innocently that if I left it up to psychologists to translate it into their own terms, they would take it from there. But when the realization came of the true gulf that separated PCT from conventional psychology (a realization due largely to people who had joined me in my efforts), it became apparent that PCT would simply have to progress on its own, not through being merged into the mainstream as I had always hoped. What research was to be done would be done without financial support. What recognition came would come only from those who quite on their own found the results interesting. In effect, the people in the Control Systems Group, as we came to call ourselves, decided to do an end-run around the mainstream.

Hence this book. Any diligent person can understand PCT. This little book has been meant as a direct introduction to the basic principles, with enough practical application to lead the interested reader into the rest of the PCT literature that now exists. The impetus behind PCT is going to come, for the next few decades, from people without any commitment to older theories. It will come from people who need a sound understanding of human behavior and have not found it in what psychology has so far managed to produce. To a great extent, PCT is going to be judged in the near future by the people who need a workable theory of behavior to teach, administer, heal, and help. The shortcomings of PCT will be described by those people, and the researchers will listen to them first.

Perhaps conventional psychologists will pay attention when they find that a different concept of behavior has appeared and is being accepted without their permission. When the leaders see which way everyone is headed, they will hurry to catch up.

The meaning of PCT will become more and more clear to you as you apply the principles in this book to everyday situations. As the title of this books suggests, PCT interprets behavior in terms of *sensory experience*, not *action*. As you see how people control their own experiences, and how you control your own, I believe you will begin to have a different attitude toward others and toward yourself. There is an enormous difference between seeing people as machines run by their environments and seeing them as self-regulating autonomous systems. I hope you will be led to want to know more; I've asked Dag Forssell (who is also, with Gregory Williams, an archivist of the Control Systems Group), to append a reading list in the Reference section. From that list you can pick materials that go more deeply into the details of the theory, other materials that illustrate how research is done in this field and which show some of the results, and still others which show how some people have begun to apply the theory.

Nothing in PCT is certain, nothing is traditional, nothing is carved in stone. This is a new venture in understanding living systems, a mere baby in the world of scientific ideas. Nobody knows how PCT will look in 10 or 20 years. But I think that the basic ideas you have learned in this book will last a bit longer than that.

Reference

Compiled and Edited by Dag Forssell

Contents

Possible Levels of Perception and Control

William T. Powers

Chapter 3 was devoted mainly to getting across the idea of levels of perception and control. The basic idea was that a higher-level system acts to control its own perception by sending reference signals to lower systems—signals that tell *them* what to perceive. This is all neat and logical, but there's another approach that isn't so neat and logical: it's the one I actually used when trying to identify levels of perception during the 40 (and more) years of developing this theory. It's not easy to identify levels in a way that will hold up to close inspection. In 40 years of trying, I've come up with 11 levels, which is less than $1/3$ of a level per year—and I've had to change my mind several times.

I will probably have to change it again.

What I'm trying to say is "Don't take these levels I propose too seriously." A lot of people talk about them, but few have tried to do any research to see if they're real. I think of them as a useful starting-point for talking about the hierarchy of control; they'll do until something better comes along.

Getting Started with the Levels

The first time I felt any sense of progress in identifying actual levels of perception came when I was considering the perceptions we call "objects." Here is an object sitting on the table in front of me. It's obviously a perception. But what is this perception made of? Here is the computer mouse: I can see its shape, and the buttons on it, and the cable coming out of it. Is that all?

Once you see an answer it's easy, but it took me a while to realize that I was asking the wrong question. What I really wanted to know is what this shape is made of *that isn't just another shape.* If I just stuck with looking at shapes, I would find myself looking at smaller and smaller shapes, down to the bump on one of the buttons, or a particular twist in the cable, or a speck of dirt (gotta wipe off that mouse). When I got to the smallest shapes I could see, I would be done, but I would still be talking about shapes, even if I started imagining shapes like molecules, atoms, and quarks. So what is a shape made of that is not another shape?

If you haven't seen the answer already, this is a good lesson in what it's like to try to analyze perceptions. You can be looking right at the answer, yet if you're observing in terms of the wrong level of perception it might as well not exist as far as conscious understanding is concerned. The answer is that the shapes are all made of sensations, which in themselves are not shapes.

My mouse is a sort of cream color (that's not a shape, I hope), but as I scan my eye over it I see that there are wide variations in shading and brightness, and even in color. There are dark lines on it where the pieces fit together; I think they're a kind of dark brown. And all around the body of the mouse, there is a blue color that is very different from the color of the mouse—it's the mouse pad on which it rests. There's a light blue color most of the way around, but a much darker blue in the shadow of the mouse. If I look very carefully at the edge where the mouse quits and the mouse pad begins, I don't really see anything—

there's no line as in a cartoon, just a place where one color stops and another begins. There's no object to see where the edge is, and it's not a color, either. It's just an impression of edgeness. Under just the right lighting conditions, I might see a "Mach Band" at the edge, but it's such a minor effect that we can ignore it.

Basically the mouse ends where a sensation turns from cream into blue. If I put the mouse on a cream-colored background, its edge would be much harder to see. If I adjusted the illumination of background just so, in fact, the mouse would disappear, except for some shadings and lines floating in space like the smile of the Cheshire Cat. If there were no differences between the sensations within the boundary of the mouse and those outside it, there would be no perception of a mouse, at least no visual perception.

This useless observation turned out to be quite useful after all. Apparently, when we perceive an object, that perception couldn't exist if there weren't different sensations of things like color and shading in the visual field. If we analyze any object or set of objects into components, and don't end up with just more and smaller objects, we end up with a collection of different sensations. The old Gestalt psychologists started down this path, but never got far with it.

Mathematically, the way we say this is that object-perceptions are functions of sensation-perceptions. Imagine a black box into which comes some set of sensation signals, and out of which comes one signal that is an object perception. If you vary the input sensations, you will continue to see the same object as long as the variations are of certain kinds. But variations of different kinds would make the object perception start fading out—you'd see less and less of it, until there was no object at all. Changing the color of the background would eventually change your ability to see the object, if the background became exactly the color of the object. Of course with other kinds of changes in sensations—their locations relative to each other, for example—you might start seeing a different object, or several different objects, but those impressions would come from *other* object-recognizers that start to wake up as the sensations change toward the distributions they are organized to detect.

The most interesting thing here is that while we can show that object perception depends on sensation perception, we can consciously experience *both* kinds of perception. I can look at the mouse and see a mouse, or I can look at the mouse and see cream and blue. And I can see a cream-and-blue mouse. So awareness isn't restricted to any one level of the hierarchy; we don't experience just the topmost level. We can experience *any* level of perception, and (within limits) more than one at a time. Don't ask me how this works; I don't know.

The general name for "object" perception is "configuration" perception, where the perception means a particular static arrangement of sensations. In the auditory mode of perception, a configuration could be something like a major chord, with the sensations of which it is made being pitches of sounds. If you vary the sensations so the different pitches change in the same ratio, the sense of a major chord stays constant. If you vary them in some other way, the major chord disappears, and perhaps some other chord-configuration begins to be heard, like a minor sixth. A trained musician can hear many different chord-configurations in a single collection of pitches. In the tactile world, a configuration might be the feel of a child's block in your hand, the sensations being such things as pressure, texture, and temperature sensations, as well as joint-angle sensations. In the taste modality, a taste-configuration like chocolate might be a function of sensations of salty, sweet, sour, and bitter. We can consciously sort some configurations into sensations more easily than others; tastes are harder than visual objects, but trained tasters can do it easily. A trained wine taster can tell you that there was a dirty sock in the vat (or at least some taste sensation that reminds her of a dirty sock).

This gives us two levels of perception, and two levels of control. To control a configuration—to turn a block so we see it corner on, for example—the actions we take consist of *altering sensations.* The shadings, edges, colors, and so on have to change until they are just right to give the appearance of a block as we look toward one corner. We *control* one level of perception by *varying* a lower level of perception. And of course to vary the lower level of perception, we must issue reference signals to control systems that act on the world to change perceptions of that level.

Thus we have two nice principles for identifying levels of perception relative to each other. A higher level of perception depends on the existence of perceptions of a lower level and can't exist without them. And to control a higher level of perception, we must *vary* perceptions of a lower level.

What lies below sensations, if anything? We can get a little help from neuroanatomy here. A sensation like warmth, it turns out, can be elicited by warming any of a large number of sensory receptors in different places on the skin. There are many more warmth receptors than different sensations of warmth, which doesn't distinguish *which* receptors were involved. So just as going from sensations to configurations involves a many-to-one transformation, so going from this lower level to sensations also involves a many-to-one transformation.

The lowest level of perception is the one that directly comes from the sensory nerve-endings. All that a sensory nerve-ending, all by itself, can report to the brain is *how much stimulation* is acting on it. If there's a small amount, the nerve signal goes blip............blip............blip, and if there's a lot it goes blipblip-blipblipblip. That's the language of nerve impulses: *how much* is represented by how fast the blips come. The nerve signal, in the language of blips, reports the *intensity of stimulation* of a single sensory nerve-ending. So we call this the level of intensity perception.

Now, looking back at my mouse, I can see that even if the whole field of view were cream-colored, I could still see the mouse if the background cream color were *brighter* or *darker* than the cream color of the mouse—if the *intensities* were different between the mouse and the background. Not only are sensations functions of intensity signals from many different sensory endings, but configurations can also be created from sets of different intensity signals, skipping the level of sensations. That's why we can see black and white pictures just as well as color pictures. Configurations are functions of sensations and intensities; sensations are functions of intensities only, since intensities are the lowest level of perception.

This gives us another principle to check out: a perception of a given level can be a function of perceptions of *any lower level*.

Just to finish this out, how do we control intensity sensations? Some of them we control directly, by contracting muscle fibers. The intensity signals that are directly affected are those representing tension in the tendons. There are also muscle-fiber-length signals generated in a somewhat more complex way; in fact I'm not quite sure what level to assign them to, if it matters.

When we control these basic intensity signals using the muscles, we also create a very large number of side-effects that affect other senses all over and inside the body. So control of intensity using muscles can also be a means of controlling other kinds of intensities—for example, light intensity, which we can control with our irises, eyelids, or oculomotor muscles. If you want to increase the intensity of a smell you can use muscles to sniff some air in; if you want to decrease it you can hold your breath. If you want to feel a greater intensity of effort, you just increase the muscle tension.

Having reached the bottom with intensity (how-much)

perceptions, we can go back upward, numbering the levels: first level, intensities. Second level, sensations. Third level, configurations. A higher-level perception can't exist without lower-level ones being present in the right combinations; to control a higher-level perception it's necessary to vary lower-level perceptions. And a perception of a given level can be a function of perceptions at any lower level. That's not a bad theoretical haul for just sitting here and looking at a computer mouse (and remembering a few helpful facts).

The Whole Array of Levels

We've worked our way down and up again to level three, configurations. Intensities, sensations, configurations. What comes next?

What is it that we perceive that depends on the existence of different configurations, sensations, and intensities? What is it that we can control only by varying intensities, sensations, or configurations? What is it that can be composed of different configurations, different sensations, or different intensities? And since the answer could include just about anything in human experience, we also have to ask, "What is the *least* step upward we can take? What kind of perception depends on these lower-level ones, with *no other levels in between?*"

That one took a while, but the answer seems fairly good: transitions.

4. Transitions.

The most familiar transition perception is what we call "motion." A series of different configurations, if they are similar enough and occur rapidly enough (but not too rapidly), introduce the sense of motion into a scene—that's what movies and television depend on. But we don't need a series of distinct steps to create a sense of motion. The second hand on a clock creates a continuing impression of rotation. A cloud drifting by gives a small perception of motion; a low-flying fighter jet gives a much larger perception of motion. In fact, just about any kind of perception from configurations to intensities can, by changing, give rise to a sense of motion. And "motion" is not the only kind of transition. When you run hot water into your lukewarm bath, you can feel the water "warming up," and it is specifically the rate of change of temperature that you sense. The pitch of a sound can be rising or falling. You may wish that a bad taste were fading from your mouth faster. "Morphing" a picture (changing one form into another continuously, as in some TV commercials and cartoons) creates a sense of transition as the shape changes, without any movement of the whole object, or any rotation. When you give your sweetie a squeeze, it is the change of pressure that conveys the affection.

From here on I will just describe the levels as I see them. Their plausibility varies a lot, and since their reality depends on reports of subjective impressions, there's nothing to "prove" here. I hope that others agree that the world comes apart in these ways, since they are supposed to be common categories of all human experience.

5. Events.

I'm not too sure about this one, but it does seem to fit the requirements. An event can't exist unless there is some set of transition, configuration, sensation, or intensity perceptions. To control an event (make it happen), you must vary transitions and so forth. And an event can consist of transitions alone, configurations alone—perceptions of any lower level in any combination. An event is a familiar space-time package of perceptions that follows one particular pattern: the bounce of a ball, the explosion of a firecracker, the opening of a door, the serve in a tennis game, a fragment of a song, a spoken word. As long as the correct set of transitions and so on is occurring, we get the sense of *the same event in progress*. I think that a "morpheme" in linguistics is an event in the sense meant here. An event has a beginning, a middle, and an end, but it is perceived as a single unitary event that occurs at one moment of time—sometimes a rather long moment, as in saying "supercallifragilisticexpialidocious." Actually, that's probably a sequence of events; it's *too* long to be perceived as a unit.

6. Relationships.

Once again we shift directions, or change the subject. Now we're talking about a perception that depends on the existence of more than one lower-level perception at the same time, and specifically on *independent* lower-level perceptions—independent except for the relationship between them. When a dog is "chasing" a cat, the relationship we perceive is "chasing." From another point of view we can also see the relationship "fleeing"—

which is logically related to chasing, but only at a higher level of perception. "Near" is one relationship, "far" is another, at this level. When one event occurs, and then another one occurs, we tend to perceive the relationship of causation: the first event causes the second event. Then we have all the prepositions which almost all refer to relationships: in, on, beside, inside, left of, above, before, at the same time as, without, bigger than, sweeter than, brighter than, more painful than, sadder than (these aren't all prepositions), surrounding, and because of. At least those. If you start looking at spatial relationships alone, you can spend all day enumerating them, starting with the relationship between your right little finger and your nose, or between your nose and the southeast corner of the room. These perceptions of relationship are created by relationship-perceivers; we can notice far more of them than we are equipped to control.

Are they real? Well, go over to where the distance between the television set and the wall is, and put your finger on it (on the distance, that is). When speaking of relationships, people begin to get the idea that the perceptions are inside of them, rather than existing in that "real external world."

7. Categories.

As I write this I'm in the middle of a long argument on the internet (See *Control Systems Group and Network*) about just what a category is, so don't expect everyone to agree with this definition. I'll just say what I think it is, as a perception.

A category is a perception that arises when any one of some

set of lower-level perceptions is present. That is, if there is a certain dog, *or* a jackknife with a particular nick in its handle, *or* a pair of worn socks, *or* a particular inflection of the voice, *or* the initials WTP present in lower-level perceptions, I experience the category, "mine." These things have nothing to do with each other, but they are all "mine." That is basically how I see categories being formed. Often they make more sense: "anything with three legs," for example. But they are basically arbitrary.

We form category perceptions, I think, in order to symbolize things. Instead of pointing to one cat, then another cat, then another thing that might be mistaken for a dog, and so on, we use the written configuration "cats," and by convention understand that this verbal configuration belongs to the same category as the set of individual, unique, configuration perceptions. I can either show you an example of the animal, or utter the word-event "cat," and you will perceive the category I intend for you to perceive because the vocal word-event also belongs to the same category.

Below this level, all the perceptions are continuously variable (with "events" being questionable, which is why I'm diffident about it). At the category level, we suddenly begin to talk in either-or terms. Either something is a cat, or it isn't. At the level of configurations we might get a bit of catness and a bit of dogness out of some odd creature at an animal show, but at that level every perception is unique. However, at the category level, we don't hesitate: it's a dog, we say. Or it's a cat. That little word "a" tells us we're talking about a category, not a specific configuration, a specific animal. In a roomful of cats, in fact, it's very difficult to refer in words to any specific animal. You have to keep adding details from lower levels of perception: the one near the south window, with white markings on black, that's chewing on the orange cat from the left side, as opposed to the one chewing on the orange cat from the right side. When you're trying to refer to a specific perception of a specific cat, you have to start looking at all the differences. When you talk about "cats," you're ignoring the differences.

When we speak or otherwise use symbols, we are referring to category perceptions almost exclusively. And of course they are categories of relationships, events, transitions, and so on.

8. Sequences.

At this level, what we perceive is ordering in time. "John hit Mary" is perceived as a different ordering from "Mary hit John." In addition, the significance of the different orderings is important to higher level systems, but this is the level where we perceive ordering per se; without this perceptual ability we would see no difference between the two sentences if they were spoken; the words would just be three events. Ordering of events makes a considerable difference; in an old calculus book, its author, speaking of the ordering of matrix operations, said "Consider the following two events: taking out liability insurance, and running your car into the car of a struggling young attorney."

A sequence is a list of perceptions that occur in a fixed order, like a recipe for baking a cake or instructions for knitting or crocheting patterns. The speed makes no difference; only the ordering matters; what happens first, second, third, and so on. You open the door and *then* go through it, not the other way around. We probably perceive and control sequence because ordering *does* make a difference.

9. Programs.

A program is a structure of tests and choice-points connecting sequences. From this innocent definition we can derive mathematics, language, logic, and all rule-driven procedures. If this perception occurs, do that step; otherwise do the other step. It is the choice-point that distinguishes a program from a sequence, the point where the if-then process could go any of several directions, depending on the states of lower-level perceptions. A picture of a program looks like a network, not a list, and you can't say what path will be followed through the network until you run the program—unless you can predict perfectly what all the lower-level perceptions will be at every choice-point.

To *control* a *perception* of a program is to vary the lower-level perceptions to keep the program going right. Long division is a nice example that we all had to learn once. There are no instructions for what numbers to write down in what order. What you write down depends on the numbers you are given. There are rules that say what to do if one number is larger or smaller than another, but you don't know what the action will be until you see the numbers that develop as the program runs. We all perceive the structure of a long-division program, but it's not any fixed sequence of actions. The program level is where we think rationally and reason out what to do to achieve our goals.

10. Principles.

These are what we are trying to maintain when we carry out specific logical or rational programs. Here is where we find honesty, and conservation of energy, and successive approximation, and safety first. We can make the logical world conform to these principles by choosing what programs of action, what reasoning processes and rules, to put into effect at a given time. A principle is no particular rule-driven process; it is something that can be exemplified by a particular process, but there are also other processes that would be equally good examples. Most principles are hard to quantify; what, exactly, constitutes a "neat" room? What particular sentences should one utter to demonstrate "candor?" What is "responsible" behavior?

Here we find moral principles and reference conditions: thou shalt not (X), where X is some generalization, rather than any specific action. The commandment does not say "Thou shalt not stick a knife in John's heart." It just says "Thou shalt not murder," and it's up to you, or someone, to decide what specific programs of action that forbids. If you have a good logical case, or a good lawyer, the jury may decide that the specific act you performed does not come under the principle of murder, but of self-defense, and home you go.

11. System Concepts.

Sets of principles are brought together into one coherent kind of perception that I call system concepts. When we speak of "government," meaning our government, we think of principles like "my country right or wrong," and "no taxation without representation," and "government of laws, not men." The system concept is the overriding idea of some organized entity; the principles at the level below are the details that make it what it is. The science of physics is a grand system concept built on most carefully crafted principles that are many and consistent with each other. Other system concepts, like "self," also grow out of sets of principles, but are seldom as well worked out as the principles of physics. Some system concepts are important and lofty, like religions, and others are perfectly mundane, like a bowling league.

If we couldn't perceive system concepts, we couldn't speak about "a person" except as an object, or a set of habits, or a set of traits. The sense of personality that one gets, different for different people, is, I think, perceived at the system concept level. When someone rants and raves about "the system," he or she is urging that we should fix an error at the system concept level.

While the behavior of people who support particular system concepts does have effects, like creating collections of rules and customs or artifacts like tools and buildings, system concepts are basically perceptions residing in the heads of the people who perceive them. If you didn't perceive and in some way support a system concept like the law, it would not exist for you. You could appreciate that it existed for other people, but it would be like understanding that some ancient race worshipped the Moon Goddess with all the principles and rules of Moon Goddess morality and customs. You might have to be wary when you're around Moon Goddess worshippers, lest you get in trouble with them, but since the perception of the Moon Goddess has no reality for you, you'd just be going through the motions. The system concepts that govern our lives the most directly are those in which we believe, that seem completely real to us, and that we will exert a lot of effort to maintain. And those that cause the most trouble between people are those that are different enough to require conflicting principles and conflicting rules.

Note that both system concepts and principles are *above* the level of rational thinking, the program level. We select and use programs in support of principles, and we select and use principles in support of system concepts.

Wrapping Up

Are there any more levels? I don't know. Are the levels defined here correct? I don't know that, either. All I can say is that this collection of levels seems to cover a very wide range of human perception and control. It brings to our attention the fact that some perceptions depend on others—a fact that would be far from obvious if we just looked at experience raw, where all the levels are mixed together and there is nothing to indicate that one is of a different type from another. It emphasizes the fact that *all* of experience is perception. This list of levels doesn't leave very much that we can just take for granted as the way the world is, "out there." And I think it gives us some direction in which to look when things go wrong.

Rather than slavishly memorizing these levels, I hope people will pay more attention to the *idea* of levels of perception. We control some kinds of perception as a way of controlling higher-level kinds; it's seldom that we control one perception just for its own sake. This whole idea of a hierarchy of perception and control is a system concept, built on principles that are built on rule-driven processes, and so on down to the bottom. Like all ideas, it's the product of a human brain or mind trying to bring order and sense into experience, to see life as being coherent, and to find overriding concepts that make it hang together, to give it beauty and worthiness and make the whole process seem worth bothering with.

WTP
July 23, 1997

An Application of PCT:
The Responsible Thinking Process

by Tom Bourbon

Discipline programs for schools are a dime a dozen, and most of them aren't worth one red cent. Discipline programs reflect the theories their creators believe, and most of them believe that behavior is an effect produced by prior causes. People who believe those cause-effect theories usually treat other people like objects whose behavior is controlled by forces beyond their own control.

That is certainly what we see in schools. People in one large group believe that reinforcement from the environment controls behavior. They use discipline programs that claim positive reinforcement allows teachers to control students' behavior. People in a second large group believe that thoughts control behavior. Some people in this group use discipline programs that claim positive aphorisms and slogans, and "cognitive exercises," allow teachers to control students' behavior. Others in this group use programs that claim teachers can control students' behavior by meeting all of their "psychological needs." People in a third major group believe that brain chemistry controls behavior. Members of that group often use discipline programs that come out of a bottle, in the form of drugs that experts say will control students' behavior.

Perceptual Control Theory (PCT), described by Bill Powers in this little book, is different from all of those traditional cause-effect theories. Powers explains that behavior is the way a person controls his or her own perceptions. There is a discipline program that reflects many of Powers's ideas. It is the Responsible Thinking Process, developed by Ed Ford (See *Applications of*

PCT in the next section). I have been studying Ford's program for the past year and a half. Let me describe a little of what I have seen.

Disturbances and Disruptions

In Ed Ford's Responsible Thinking Process (RTP), a disruption at school is understood as an instance where one student, who is controlling his own perceptions, disturbs perceptions controlled by someone else. Sometimes one person intends to disturb another, but many times the disturbances are accidental; they are unintended side effects that occur while the "disrupter" focuses attention on the perceptions he intends to control. In either case, Ford says the problem is not the disrupter's *behavior*, for, as Powers showed in this book, when people control perceptions, they are often unaware of their behavioral actions. Instead, the problems are the disturbance those actions cause for another person, and the conflict that often follows the disturbance.

Ford's RTP produces effects like some of those in the method of "going up a level" that Powers described in this book. The RTP is designed to draw a disrupting student's attention away from his immediate controlled perceptions, to the consequences of his actions for other people, and to how his actions relate to the rules for how people should interact at school. In RTP, the rules are guidelines that let students know how they can control their own perceptions without unnecessarily disturbing others, and how they can resolve conflicts that occur when they do disturb others.

Questions and the RTC

When a student disrupts, the teacher asks a few simple questions, in a calm and respectful voice:

"What are you doing?"
"What is the rule?," or *"Is that OK?"*
"What happens if you break the rule?"
"Is that what you want to happen?"
"What will happen the next time you disrupt?"

The questions afford a choice to a student who disrupts: either he can stop disrupting and remain in the class, or he can continue to disrupt, and thereby choose to leave the classroom and go to the Responsible Thinking Classroom (RTC). For students who stop disrupting when they answer the questions the first time, nothing else happens. After teachers use the RTP for a while, the first question is often all they need. When they hear that question, most students who are disrupting immediately stop and indicate that they understand what they are doing and how it violates guidelines for the ways people should treat one another. On the other hand, if a student continues to disrupt after hearing the questions the first time, the teacher says, calmly, "I see you have chosen to go to the RTC."

In the RTC, the same rules apply as in the regular classroom, and the RTC teacher uses the same questioning procedure with students who disrupt. If students disrupt the RTC, they go home. Schools cannot provide an infinite number of places for students; either they are in class, or they are in the RTC. In RTP, the choice of where to be always remains with the student.

While they are in the RTC, Ford says students can sit quietly, or read, or do homework, or sleep. They can do anything, so long as they do not disrupt the RTC. Whenever a student decides she is ready, she works on a plan for how to return to class.

In her written plan, the student describes what she did to disrupt the class, and works out a strategy that she thinks will help her avoid a similar situation in the future. The idea is for a student to learn how to control her own perceptions without unnecessarily disturbing other people while they control their perceptions. Some plans say the student will sit somewhere else in the classroom, away from her friends, or that she will ask a friend to help her through situations where she has had problems. Other plans say the student will ignore students who try to provoke him into disrupting, or that he will ask for a pass to go to the RTC whenever he feels like he is "losing control." There are many kinds of plans, and all of them are prepared by the students. The RTC teacher can help with a plan if a student requests assistance. When a student decides her plan is ready, then the RTC teacher looks through it to be sure it addresses all of the necessary subjects.

When the RTC teacher and the student agree that the written plan is ready, the student presents it to the classroom teacher, or to the person in charge of the area the student disrupted. The adult reads the student's plan and the two of them negotiate any points on which they disagree, or on which the teacher thinks the student might want to consider other options. When both of them are satisfied, the student returns to class.

That is the core of Ford's program. It is used in schools in at least eight states, and in Australia and Germany. It is used with students in grades from pre-kindergarten through high school. Some of the high schools are traditional, some are alternative schools, and some are in prisons for juveniles. The only consideration given to grade levels is that the questions and plans are simpler for children in primary grades. Also, if they disrupt twice, younger students go to a secluded place in the classroom, rather than to the RTC. The program is used successfully with all students, including ones "diagnosed" with various intellectual or emotional "disabilities."

The RTP is used in schools where more than 90 percent of the students are White, and others where more than 90 percent are Hispanic, or Native American. It is used in schools where the largest percentage of students is Black, or Asian. It is used in "tough," inner-city schools, in suburban schools, and in isolated rural schools. It is used in affluent schools, and in schools where more than 80 percent of the students qualify for free meals, or meals at reduced cost.

A Brief Review of Results
Observations

A frequent comment from the faculty in a school where RTP succeeds is: "Everything is so much quieter and calmer. Everyone is so much more relaxed" That is exactly what I have seen during visits to schools.

Before I started observing Ford's program, I spent 27 years in universities, overlapping with 11 years in medical schools. I had no idea what I would see in K-12 schools. When I visited the first several schools that used RTP, I thought to myself: "They set me up. They picked schools that never had a problem." No matter the time of day when I arrived, there were no students waiting to be disciplined by administrators. Often, I could talk for an hour or more with the administrator in charge of discipline, and not a single incident required the person's attention. I saw that phenomenon many times.

Before my visits, I thought many students might want to avoid regular classes and spend all of their time in RTC, but instead, 95 percent to 98 percent of the students who go to the RTC want to return to the regular classroom in the same day. I also wondered if RTP might produce students who behaved like "mindless robots," sitting stiff and silent in their seats. Nothing could be further from what I saw in the schools. In cafeterias, on playgrounds, and in hallways, I saw students who were animated and pleasant, but who did not fight or try to bother others. I saw classrooms in which everyone was calm and "on task." I stood in hallways for hours, listening for the shouting and yelling that everyone told me I would have heard before the school started to use RTP. When someone did disrupt, I heard teachers ask "the questions," calmly and inquisitively.

Many teachers told me, sometimes with tears in their eyes, that they were teaching their subjects for the first time in many years, or that they had been ready to leave teaching before their school started to use RTP. Teachers and administrators told me, excitedly, about how they have implemented curriculum changes and innovative programs that they could not even talk about, when discipline was a major problem in their school.

I have talked with many students and read many student surveys, some from very young children. In the language of a young child in Michigan, a common theme is, "It (RTP) is good for kids. It helps bullies not be bullies any more, but they don't really get in trouble. It helps them learn to be nicer." A young former "bully" in Texas said, "It (the RTC) was good for me. Now I don't pick on other kids at school and I don't fight at home anymore. My mother likes that." Many students at a rough high school in Arizona said that, in RTP, they were being treated with respect at school for the first time they could remember.

I discovered another interesting way to gauge students' opinions about the RTC. Most schools hold "parents' nights" or "open houses," when parents visit the schools, often with their children. On those nights, I doubt that many students ever take their parents to visit a detention hall or an in-school suspension room, but they do take them to visit the RTC. One evening at an elementary school in Arizona, 25 students took their parents to RTC, to show them where they got help so they wouldn't have problems at school. At a high school in a juvenile prison, nine young men took their parents or guardians to RTC and told them, "This is where they helped me straighten myself out." One young man who successfully worked his way out of an alternative high school in Michigan brought his girlfriend back to see the RTC and he told her, "This is where I finally got myself together." Those unsolicited testimonials speak eloquently to the nature of what happens in the RTC. Students might not want to go there, and they might say it is a boring place, but they view the RTC as a "safe haven" and a place where they receive help.

Data

There are data to support my observations. Here are a few examples. Ford's RTP was developed at a school in Phoenix, Arizona (4th - 6th grade). In the first year of the program, compared to the year before, physical assaults declined 62 percent, possession of weapons declined 100 percent, fighting incidents declined 69 percent, and incidents of theft declined 27 percent. In the first year of RTP at a school in Illinois (K - 5th grade), "serious acts of misbehavior" declined by 65 percent from the previous year. During the last four months of the year, external suspensions were an average 66 percent below the previous year.

At a correctional facility (prison) for juvenile males in Arizona, the high school began to use RTP in 1997. During the first four months of 1997, compared to the same period in 1996, disruptions decreased 52 percent in the school and 42 percent in the remainder of the facility. During the first year and a half when a "tough" high school in Arizona used RTP, there was a decline in disruptions and vandalism on the campus, and academic performance increased.

Special Education

Ed Ford's RTP has been used successfully with many special education students whose "diagnoses" are intended to imply that the children cannot tell right from wrong, or that they cannot learn to "control their own actions." In a pre-kindergarten class in Arizona, the children wear a wide array of diagnostic labels. They learn to answer questions like, "What did my eyes see your hands do? Is that OK? Is there a way you can play with the doll and not take it away from Tim?" At another school in Arizona, a class with children between five and eight years old also houses children with various diagnostic labels. The teacher uses augmentative devices, like pictures on the wall or speech synthesizers, to help nonverbal students identify what they did to disrupt the class, and to help them select a plan for how to avoid disrupting again. Children who continue to disrupt go to the RTC, perhaps accompanied by a private attendant and the equipment to meet their special physical needs. There are no exceptions to the RTP program in that school.

In schools that use RTP, very young students with special needs demonstrate that they know when they took a toy from another child. They also select plans that call for them to share toys, or to take turns playing with them. Those students know when they have hit someone else, and they select plans that call for them to keep their hands to themselves, or to move away from people they might hit. What is more, the students are eager and proud to show the teacher, or visitors, that they are following their plans. Those students do not conform to what experts say they can and cannot do, or to what teachers were trained to expect from them, or to what their parents came to believe were their limitations.

At a school in Texas, many emotionally-disturbed students had spent several years in special units, without ever returning to the regular classroom. A few months after RTP was introduced into their units, some of those students were in regular classrooms for three or more periods each day. At a school in Mississippi, a young man diagnosed with autism and four other major disorders was referred to a special unit that had just started to use RTP. When he arrived in the unit, he disrupted his class so often that he made as many as six visits a day to the room that was equivalent to the RTC. By the end of the year, the young man went to the special room no more than once every two or three weeks.

Time and again, teachers who use RTP with special education students discover that the children can do much more than mental health professionals believe. Often, it becomes clear that traditional diagnoses create expectations that everyone helps the students meet. Thus, a student in Michigan, diagnosed with "attention deficit hyperactivity disorder," was said to be "so out of control that he cannot function unless the teacher stands next to him." In fact, the young man was controlling the teacher's behavior by "making" the teacher stand where the student wanted him to stand. When the student was treated like all others in the Responsible Thinking Process, he quickly "gained control over his own actions."

Similarly, when a disruptive autistic student was allowed to go to the RTC, he remained there quietly for a while. He decided to return to the classroom, and he made a plan to do so. Had the staff tried to prevent that student from leaving the regular classroom, he would have behaved as though he wanted to leave and to be alone; he would have confirmed traditional ideas about what autistic children do and why they do it.

Frequent Flyers

After RTP begins to work well in a school, an interesting phenomenon appears. Most students in the school never go to the RTC, and only a few students go there very often. The latter are often called "frequent flyers." In some schools, many teachers decide that frequent flyers prove that RTP does not work, and they revert to using various rewards and punishments to control students' behavior. When they do that, RTP is no longer in effect and discipline problems become more serious.

There are some interesting data concerning frequent flyers. As an example of the phenomenon, let us look closely at data from the juvenile correctional facility in Arizona, during May 1997.

Total youth in facility	132	
Youth who went to RTC	58	(44% of all students)
Total visits to RTC	122	
1 or 2 visits to RTC	33 students	(25% of all students, 37% of all visits)
4 to 8 visits to RTC	7 students	(5% of all students 30% of all visits)

During that month, seven young men accounted for 30 percent of all visits to the RTC, and the staff knew about extraordinary circumstances for each of the seven. The young men were using the RTC as a safe and stable place, where they could control their perceptions of difficult circumstances in their lives.

My data show that, when faculties become disturbed by "all of those students who make frequent visits to RTC," they are usually talking about very few students. At the school in Illinois, there are 700 students. During all of 1996-97, 15 students (2% of all students) made 32% of all visits to the RTC. A school in Arkansas (K - 6th grade) started using RTP in 1996-97. There are 615 students, a majority of whom never went to the RTC. Only 15 students (2% of all students) made over one-third of the total visits to the RTC. A middle school (4th - 8th grade) in Arizona started RTP in 1995. During 1996-97, there were 560 students in the school, of whom 256 (46%) never went to the RTC. Only 16 students (3% of all students) made a third of all visits to the RTC during the year.

The way that faculty members deal with "frequent flyers" depends on how well they understand the basic principles of

RTP, and of Perceptual Control Theory. In some schools, the faculty literally destroys RTP in an attempt to "make all of those students stop going to the RTC so often." Using the logic from cause-effect theories of behavior, they believe RTP should "fix" the students, or the school, so that no one will ever disrupt again. Those adults do not understand that everyone acts to control perceptions, and sometimes they cannot avoid disturbing others. They sacrifice the entire RTP program because they want to completely control the behavior of the most troubled two percent to five percent of the students. In the process, they ignore the large majority of students who do not disrupt at all, or who disrupt only once or twice a year.

When people understand the basic concepts of RTP, they interpret frequent trips to the RTC as evidence that a student is trying to control perceptions of a serious problem in his or her life. The adults then devote special attention and resources to helping the "frequent flyer" make it through a difficult time. Ed Ford recommends that frequent visits to the RTC call for an "intervention team" to determine what is happening in the student's life, and how to help the student. The intervention team comprises people who might offer insights into the child's life or who might be able to help the child through a difficult time. It might include people such as the RTC teacher, teachers or members of the school staff who have detailed knowledge about the student or with whom the student feels comfortable, the student's parent(s) or guardian(s), and resource people from the school (such as a counselor or psychologist) or from the community (such as a probation officer or case worker).

Some of the problems uncovered by intervention teams are horrendous. A student in an elementary school disrupted to go to the RTC as a safe place, following weekends when his older brother had sold him as a sex toy to older men—the same older brother had anally raped the young boy, some time earlier. The courts decreed that a student in another elementary school should live with his mother, but that his father should assist with the boy's schooling. The boy desperately wanted to be with his father; he disrupted often, in order to create times when his father would come to school with him. In another school, children from one family made frequent trips to the RTC after their father murdered their mother, in their presence. The children went to live with their grandparents. The next year, they made frequent visits to the RTC after their grandfather murdered their grandmother, in their presence.

There are equally terrible stories behind many students who make frequent visits to the RTC. Ed Ford's RTP helps identify students who are at special risk, and it affords a process to help them regain control of their own perceptions during extremely difficult times.

Conclusion

Many people wonder if it makes a difference to think about people as though they were living perceptual control systems. From what I have seen in schools that successfully use Ed Ford's Responsible Thinking Process, it makes a *big* difference.

Studies in PCT

Readings

Introductory College Text

Introduction to Modern Psychology: The Control Theory View

Robertson, Richard J. and Powers, William T., Eds. (1990)

A primary text for introductory college-level psychology courses and for independent study. IL: First edition, Lillemor Publishing. Second edition in press, Benchmark Publications Inc., 1998.

Several of the other books, demos and programs in this listing may serve as introductory texts, depending on individual interest.

Introductions to PCT Theory

Behavior: The Control of Perception

William T. Powers, (1973). This is the basic text on PCT. Fifth printing, 1998. NY: Aldine de Gruyter.

From the original book jacket:

"Powers' *Behavior: The Control of Perception* gives social scientists—finally—an alternative to both behaviorism and psychoanalysis. It provides a way, both elegant and sophisticated, to include the basic contributions of both without being partisan or converted. It allows us to bring the soma, culture, society, behavior, and experience into a single framework. We now know much more than we did before this book was published."

—Paul J. Bohannan, Stanley G. Harris Professor of Social Science, Northwestern University; author of *Divorce and After, Social Anthropology*, and other books.

"The highly original thesis of this remarkable book is deceptively simple: that our perceptions are the only reality we can know, and that the purpose of all our actions is to control the state of this perceived world. This simple thesis represents a sharp break with most traditional interpretations of human behavior. The theory set forth and developed in detail in this book proposes a testable model of behavior based on feedback relationships between organism and environment, which can reconcile the conflict between behaviorists and humanists and for the first time put us on the road to an understanding of ourselves that is at once scientific and humane.

The model advanced here explains a range of phenomena from the simplest response of a sensory nerve cell to the construction of a code of ethics, using cybernetic concepts to provide a physical explanation not only for physical acts but also for the existence of goals and purposes. A hierarchical structure of neurological control systems is proposed that is at least potentially identifiable and testable, in which each control system specifies the behavior of lower level systems and thus controls its own perceptions.

The model incorporates the "programming" of behavior in the course of human evolutionary history, the nature and significance of memory, and the reorganizations of behavior brought about by education and experience.

Written with verve and wit, with many illuminating examples and interesting thought questions, *Behavior: The Control of Perception* may well prove to be one of the truly seminal works of our time; at least, this is suggested by the distinguished scholars who read the manuscript in advance of publication (see back cover).

The book suggests many new interpretations of neurological, behavioral, and social data, an immense range of new experiments that will modify the model advanced here, and much new insight into such crucial psychological and social processes as education, the resolution of conflict, and the problems of mental illness.

About the author

William T. Powers received his B.S. in physics and did his graduate work in psychology at Northwestern University. He has consulted for The Center for the Teaching Profession, and was formerly Chief Systems Engineer of the Department of Astronomy at Northwestern. He has published articles in psychology, astronomy and electronics, and has invented and designed a number of electronic instruments."

The Nature of Robots

Powers, William T., A series of illustrated articles outline Powers' suggested organization of the human nervous system.

1 *Defining Behavior*
BYTE 4(6), June 1979, 132-144, 7p.

2 *Simulated Control System*
BYTE 4(7), July 1979, 134-152, 12p.

3 *A Closer Look at Human Behavior*
BYTE 4(8), Aug 1979, 94-116, 16p.

4 *Looking for Controlled Variables*⟩
BYTE 4(8), Sept. 1979, 96-112, 13p.

Living Control Systems: Selected Papers

Powers, William T., (1989). 14 previously published papers 1960-1988. First edition, The Control Systems Group, 1989. Second edition, CT: Benchmark Publications Inc.

Living Control Systems, Volume II: Selected Papers

Powers, William T., (1992). 22 Previously unpublished papers 1959-1990. First edition, The Control Systems Group, 1989. Second edition, CT: Benchmark Publications Inc.

PCT Demonstrations and Texts

Self-extracting DOS files with tutorial programs, functional DOS computer simulations, explanations and sizzling discussion on many subjects from the archives of CSGnet.

Available on diskette from CA: Purposeful Leadership. Download from

`http://www.forssell.com`

`ftp://burkep.libarts.wsu.edu/csg`

See also videos featuring the rubber-band demonstration and Rick Marken's web site with demonstrations programmed in the Java language.

Research

Casting Nets and Testing Specimens

Runkel, Philip J., (1990). When statistics are appropriate; when functional models are required. With explanation of PCT. New York: Praeger.

Mind Readings: Experimental Studies of Purpose

Marken, Richard S., (1992). This is a book that can show a willing psychologist how to do a new kind of research. The theme that runs through all these papers is modeling, the ultimate way of finding out what a theory really means. Richard Marken finds the essence of a problem and an elegantly simple way to cast it in the form of a demonstration or an experiment. CA: Life Learning Associates.

Purposeful Behavior: The Control Theory Approach

Marken, Richard S. (Ed.). (1990). 11 papers on PCT.
American Behavioral Scientist, 34(1). CA: Sage Publications.

A Science of Purpose:

Research Method for Control Theory

Control Theory and Statistical Generalization

Learning and Attention in Control Systems

The behavioral development of free-living chimpanzee infants

Plooij, Frans X, (1984). A description of observational studies of the development of chimpanzee babies in the wild. The data are interpreted in terms of the hierarchical model of perceptual control. NJ: Ablex.

On the accuracy and reliability of predictions by control-system theory

Bourbon, WT, KE Copeland, VR Dyer, WK Harman & BL Mosely (1990). Perceptual and Motor Skills, vol 71, 1990, 1331-1338. The first of a 20-year series demonstrating the long-term reliability and stability of predictions generated by the PCT model.

Perceptual Control Theory

Bourbon, W. Thomas (1995). Chapter 8: In Herbert L. Roitblat & Jean-Arcady Meyer, Eds.: *Comparative Approaches to Cognitive Science*. Cambridge, Mass: A Bradford Book, The MIT Press, pages 151-172. The PCT model is contrasted with some of the mainstream models and theories.

Purposeful Behavior as the Control of Perception: Implications for Educational Research

Cziko, Gary A., *Educational Researcher*, 21:9, (Nov. 92), pp.10-18; 25-27.

One threat to educational research not (yet?) faced by
Amundson, Serlin, and Lehrer

Cziko, Gary A. (1992). Perceptual Control Theory: *Educational Researcher,*
21(9), 25-27. Response to critics of previous article.

Volitional Action: Conation and Control

Hershberger, Wayne. (Ed.). (1989). (Advances in Psychology No. 62). 16 of
25 articles on or about PCT. NY: North-Holland.

Perceptual Control and Social Power

McClelland, Kent., *Sociological Perspectives,* (24 pages. Dec 1994).

Collective Control of Perceptions: Toward a Person-Centered
Sociology

McClelland, Kent., Midwestern Sociological Society Meetings (1997)

Dept. of Sociology, Grinnell College, Grinnell, IA, 50112.

The Myth of the Madding Crowd

McPhail, Clark., (1990). Introduces PCT to explain group behavior. NY:
Aldine de Gruyter.

Simulating Individual and Collective Action
in Temporary Gatherings

McPhail, Clark., William T. Powers, and Charles W. Tucker, Computer
simulation of control systems in groups. Social Science Computer Review,
10:1, (1992) pp. 1-28. NC: Duke University Press.

The Dilemma of Inquiry and Learning

Petrie, Hugh G. (1981). IL: University of Chicago Press.

Applications of PCT

Discipline for Home and School

Edward E. Ford, book I (1994-7) and book II (1996) These books describe a practical, easy-to-use program that teaches school personnel and parents how to deal effectively with children. AZ: Brandt Publishing.

Management and Leadership: Insight for Effective Practice

Forssell, Dag C., Collection of articles (1993-1996) explain and illustrate PCT and Hierarchical PCT and show how to apply an understanding based on PCT to business issues. CA: Purposeful Leadership.

Effective Personnel Management: An Application of PCT

Soldani, James. See *Volitional Action: Conation and Control* p. 515-29.

Why They Cry

Hetty van de Rijt and Frans X. Plooij, (1996) Child development book outlining the growth of nine levels of perception during the first year. Thorsons, London. Tel: +44 181 307 4403, Fax: +44 181 307 4629.

Freedom From Stress

Ford, Edward E., (1989). A comprehensive case study, written in simple, conversational language with role plays and simple illustrations. AZ: Brandt Publishing.

Love Guaranteed; a better marriage in 8 weeks

Ford, Edward E., (1987). The first applications text, explaining PCT through discussions of everyday problems and relationships. An excellent companion to the later *Freedom From Stress*. AZ: Brandt Publishing.

The Death of Jeffrey Stapleton: Exploring the Way Lawyers Think

Gibbons, Hugh., (1990). Using PCT to explain how lawyers think. Franklin Pierce Law Center, Concord, NH, 03301.

Videos Illustrating or Introducing PCT

Perceptual Control Theory

Powers, William T., (1987) Four 30 min. segments: *Feedback, Perceptions & Goals, Levels of Control, Interaction Among Control Systems.* (VHS, NTSC). AZ: Brandt Publishing.

PCT at AERA 1995

Hugh Petrie, Bill Powers, Gary Cziko, Ed Ford and Dag Forssell discuss PCT at American Education Research Association Annual Conference. Bill Powers presents the rubber band experiment. (VHS, NTSC, 120 min). CA: Purposeful Leadership

PCT Supports TQM

Forssell, Dag C., (1993) Video presentation. (VHS, NTSC, 117 min). CA: Purposeful Leadership

Rubber Band Demonstration

Forssell, Dag C., (1993). With illustrated script. (VHS, NTSC, 63 min). CA: Purposeful Leadership

Love Guaranteed

Ford, Edward E., (1992) KAET-TV (PBS), Phoenix. 46 min (VHS, NTSC) A graphically illustrated PCT view of relationships and relationship building. AZ: Brandt Publishing.

CSG Annual Conference Video Tapes: 1993, 1994, 1996, 1997.

CSG conferences are very informal. Tapes are ° inch, VHS, NTSC, EP speed. CA: Purposeful Leadership.

Control Systems Group and Network

The Control Systems Group

The CSG is an organization of people who see the potential in PCT for increased understanding in their own fields and for the unification of diverse and fragmented specialties. For information write:

CSG, c/o Mary Powers, 73 Ridge Place CR 510, Durango, CO 81301-8136
E-mail: powers_w@frontier.net.

Accessing and Subscribing to CSGnet

To subscribe to CSGnet, and learn about options & commands and archives, send a message to:

Address:	LISTSERV@POSTOFFICE.CSO.UIUC.EDU
Message:	(Comments: Not part of your message)
Subscribe CSGnet	Firstname Lastname (Your OWN name!)
help	(Basic introduction to commands)
info refcard	(Comprehensive list of commands)
set CSGnet digest	(All mail delivered once a day)
set CSGnet repro	(Get copy of your own postings)
query CSGnet	(Your mail status & options)
set CSGnet ack	(Get acknowledgments when posting)
index CSGnet	(List of archive files)
get CSGnet LOG9802B	(Get archive for 2nd week of February, 1998 - example only)

Messages to the entire CSGnet community should be addressed to:	CSGnet@POSTOFFICE.CSO.UIUC.EDU

Books Placing PCT in Context

Feedback Thought in Social Science and Systems Theory

Richardson, George P., (1991). Historical review of systems thinking, including PCT, pages 240-263. University of Pennsylvania Press.

Without Miracles:
Universal selection theory and the second Darwinian evolution

Cziko, Gary, (1995). Chap 8, "Adapted Behavior as the Control of Perception" Cambridge: MIT Press/A Bradford Book.

PCT Web Sites

Powers: http://www.frontier.net/~powers_w/

Ford: http://www.respthink.com/

Bourbon: http://www.tombourbon.com/

Forssell: http://www.forssell.com/

Marken: http://home.earthlink.net/~rmarken/

CSG: http://www.ed.uiuc.edu/csg/

Publishers

CT: Benchmark Publications Inc.

65 Locust Avenue, New Canaan, CT 06840-5328 USA
Tel: (203) 966-6653.
E-mail: benchmark@benchpress.com
http://www.benchpress.com

Phone orders: 800-559-6653 (US) or 203-966-6653 (International)
FAX: 203-972-7129

AZ: Brandt Publishing

Edward E. Ford 10209 North 56th Street, Scottsdale, AZ 85253-1130 USA
Telephone & Fax: (602) 991-4860. E-mail: edford@edford.com

CA: Purposeful Leadership

Dag Forssell 23903 Via Flamenco, Valencia, CA 91355-2808 USA
Tel: (805) 254-1195 Fax: (805) 254-7956. E-mail: dag@forssell.com

CA: Life Learning Associates

Rick Marken 10459 Holman Avenue, Los Angeles, CA 90024 USA
Tel: (310) 474-0313. E-mail: rmarken@earthlink.net

IL: Lillemor Publishing

Dick Robertson 1352 Sanford Lane, Glenview, IL 60025-3165 USA
Tel: (847) 998-8398 Fax: (847) 998-8499. E-mail: R-Robertson@neiu.edu

NY: Aldine de Gruyter

200 Saw Mill River Road, Hawthorne, NY 10532 USA
Phone orders: (914) 747-0110 Fax: (914) 747-1326

CT: Praeger

Praeger Publishers, P.O. Box 5007, Westport, CT 06881
Tel: (800) 225-5800, (203) 226-3571. Fax (203) 222-1502

CA: Sage Publications

Journal Marketing, 2455 Teller Rd, Newbury Park, CA 91320 USA
Phone orders: (805) 499-0721 Fax: (805) 499-0871

Previews of other books by WTPowers

Living Control Systems

Selected Papers of William T. Powers

On Purpose

...In trying to understand why behavior is so variable, we look closely at the details, and find a puzzle. While the general outcomes of behavior often repeat well enough for us to study them, the actions that bring about these outcomes vary almost at random.... There's a kink in the causal chain.

Organisms produce specific outcomes, not specific actions: Their actions adjust according to the momentary requirements of the environment, so that when all the influences on the outcome are added up (including the influences created by the organism), the same result appears. That is what makes behavior seem purposive. Organisms don't just go through the motions like automata; they vary their actions in whatever way is needed to achieve the results we recognize as behavior.

...When you think of a behavioral outcome as a physicist would, you see immediately that actions must vary if that outcome is to repeat. That is because other forces and constraints are always acting on the same outcome. If the independent influences change but the outcome doesn't, physics demands and reason deduces that the action must have changed, too, precisely and quantitatively the correct way. Observation confirms this expectation in essentially every instance of behavior.

Neither physics nor reason is influenced by mere beliefs: If actions systematically oppose disturbances, that is all there is to it, they do. There is then nothing to keep an engineer using physics and reason from wondering how a system has to be organized to behave that way, discovering how, and building some examples to learn more about the principles of such from organizations.

Living Control Systems II

Selected Papers of William T. Powers

After Galileo

...[Runkel's book] told us about two methods that scientists use to study behavior: the method of relative frequencies and the method of specimens. While both methods have been used formally or informally since the beginning of history, the method of specimens has become workable as a way of understanding behavior only in the last 50 years. The method of specimens requires studying one individual at a time through making models of that individual's organization and testing them against real behavior. We're just learning how to use that method as successfully in the life sciences as the physical sciences have used it for 300 years or so.

The method of relative frequencies pays almost no attention to individuals—either individual persons or individual instances of any natural phenomenon. It's the basis of empiricism; before Galileo it was essentially the only reliable basis for understanding most of nature. All it means is learning from experience. You watch what happens around you—then you try to figure out the rules....That isn't science? No, I say, it isn't. The method of relative frequencies has had a fair trial. It has been developed about as far as it can go. And it still has not produced anything that will help the human race survive its own internal conflicts and its own ignorance of human nature It could be carried on for another three hundred years without producing anything better than what we now have—except that if a real science of life is delayed that long, there may be nobody left in any condition to say that it's time to try something else.

Now, what is it that the physical sciences do differently? In Runkel's terms, the physical sciences use the method of specimens....I say they make models. A physicist tries to imagine what there might be underneath observation that would *necessarily* result in the phenomena we can see and feel. The key word here, and the key to the whole method of model building, is "necessarily."

Behavior: The Control of Perception
William T. Powers

Aldine de Gruyter, fifth printing, 1998

"Here is a profound and original book with which every psychologist—indeed every behavioral scientists—should be acquainted. It is delightful to have a person of such varied and unorthodox background come forth with a unique theory of the way in which behavior is controlled in and by the individual, a theory which should spark a great deal of significant research."
—Carl R. Rogers, Resident Fellow of the Center for Studies of the Person, La Jolla, California, Past President of the American Psychological Association and recipient of its Distinguished Scientific Contribution Award

"Powers' manuscript, *Behavior: The Control of Perception*, is among the most exciting I have read in some time. The problems are of vast importance, and not only to psychologists; the achieved synthesis is thoroughly original; and the presentation is often convincing and almost invariably suggestive. I shall be watching with interest what happens to research in the directions to which Powers points."
—Thomas S. Kuhn, Professor of the History of Science, Princeton University, author of *The Structure of Scientific Revolutions*.

Publisher's Special Offer - *POWERS on PCT*

		(s/h: book rate)
Behavior: The Control of Perception	$45.00	$4.50
Living Control Systems	$19.95	$3.50
Living Control Systems II	$19.95	$3.50
Making Sense of Behavior:	$14.95	$3.50
The Meaning of Control		
Introduction to Modern Psychology:	$25.00	$3.50
The Control Theory View		
All five volumes:	$112.50	$7.50

CT residents add 6% tax

Name _____

Address _____

City/State/ZIP _____

Phone _____Fax _____

E-mail _____

Ship to (if different) _____

City/State/ZIP _____

Credit Card (circle one)   MC   DC   VISA   AX   Expires: ___/___

Card Number _____

Cardholder's Signature _____

Cardholder's Name (print) _____

Send your check or money order to Benchmark Publications Inc.
P.O. Box 1594 - New Canaan, Connecticut 06840-5328 (U.S. funds)

FAX your credit card order to: 203-972-7129

Phone credit card orders to: 800-559-6653 (USA) or 203-966-6653.

Call or write to the listed publishers for other titles in the PCT library.